AF342212

THE HEART OF SELLING

Jim DuVal

KENDALL/HUNT PUBLISHING COMPANY
Dubuque, Iowa

B   403201   01

Contents

Thoughts of the Author

Who are you? Are you just a reflection of what other people want you to be or are you what you want to be?

What are you doing? Are you doing what other people want you to do and expect of you, or are you doing what you want to do?

How are you doing it? With natural joy and enthusiasm—or out of dread and fear?

Who stands as your judge? Are you living to be judged by your fellow man or are you willing to be your own judge—making your own choices and evaluations?

Day to day, month to month, year to year, too many people's lives just seem to be slipping away because of a lack of selfishness. They live as their parents, friends, and spouses tell them they should live rather than as they choose to live. This attitude, too often, has a negative effect on sales. Effective selling can only be based on clear personal motivation—what *you* want to do.

Why should everything you do have to be based on the value systems of others? Where is *your* self? When did it get lost? Why? Do you think so little of yourself that you would rather be judged by others?

As I travel around this country I see more and more people struggling with life because of their inability to cope with self, and they therefore look to externals for satisfaction. The results are insignificant productivity and insignificant lives which could have been meaningful, had a little selfishness been applied.

My promise to myself is that I will be productive in this lifetime, and I hope that each and every one of you will make this same promise to yourself. But I do not want to pull you and I do not want to push you. I only hope that through my writings and my teachings I will lead you to the way that's right for you.

I don't write for your approval. I hope we share a reality. What could be more worthless than to be without a self?

Jim DuVal

Introduction

*"One would need to be a God to decide which
are the failures and which are the successes
in this life."*
—Anton Chekhov

When you started in real estate sales, however recent or long ago that was, you had a particular vision and hope. Perhaps it was to make a lot of money, or manage your own time, or be independent and successful. A number of things may have happened since then—the hope or vision may have been realized, and/or it may have changed; or it may have become clouded and forgotten, or you may be wondering just why it hasn't happened—yet.

This book is for every sales person who came to real estate sales with a vision—whether realized or not. You'll have the opportunity, as you read and work through this book, to recapture and reexamine that original vision; to look at how you were or were not able to attain it; and how you can use that information to create new horizons and promises for yourself. In the process, you'll have a chance to determine for yourself—*what is success?*

Building on the experience of many successful sales associates and an immense amount of psychological and marketing research, you'll be able to apply to your life the following basics for sales success: the latest techniques for rejection-free prospecting; an understanding of your own self-image—your strengths, weaknesses, and how to overcome image problems that get in the way of your success; effective communication strategies to use with prospects, buyers, sellers, general business contacts, and everyone else in your life; and finally, a time management and goal setting program that will help you clearly define what you want and how to get it.

The *Heart of Selling* will help you get to the very core of what you can do to be the most successful person you know. It will help you define *your* success, not just with your mind but also with your feelings . . . what feels "right" for you.

As you probably know, real estate sales are built on emotion; a buyer has a certain positive response to a home and you sell to that desire. What people often overlook is the "other side of the coin"—*your* emotions and desires. What is it you want for yourself? Knowing this, building on it, and bringing that enthusiasm and commitment to your entire life is the spark that breeds success.

That's what this book is about—getting to the "heart" of the matter, discovering your desires and motivation, and building on that awareness as your source of inspiration in defining what you will do with your life from this day on and how you will do it.

This book is divided into five chapters: Self Image, Communications, Goals and Time Management, Prospecting, and Useful Tips, Lists and Readings. The first four chapters give you useful information; the final chapter provides an opportunity to make self applications of everything presented. You may choose to do this at the end of each chapter or wait until you've completed all of them, using it as a general review *and* application. Do whatever is most comfortable and useful for you.

Note: You may find that some of the information and ideas presented are new, unfamiliar, or at times, unacceptable. However, allow yourself to at least consider these ideas. Determine if they are useful for you or not by trying the following four steps:

First, DUPLICATE the information discussed, digest it, take a picture of it. (Visualize what has been presented—how would it look?)

Second, UNDERSTAND the information through your present set of experiences. (See how it would apply in various circumstances.)

Third, EVALUATE what you have understood; decide what will work for you on the basis of where you are now . . . in the future.

Fourth, CREATE your own way of acting and utilizing what you have learned. (Modify it, color it, adapt it to your style.)

By following these four steps you will be able to suspend your natural defenses which often promote denial and rejection of new ideas. Most people's first tendency, when confronted with something new, is to reject the information before it is truly understood. This is how we protect ourselves from the difficulty of change—unfortunately at the cost of learning what may be helpful to our growth.

So remember . . . duplicate,
                     understand,
                     evaluate,
                     create.

Chapter 1

Self-Image

Introduction

You've probably heard that the major pitfall for any sales associate is a negative self-image. Quite simply, a negative self-image is information you give yourself at the feeling level not founded on the here and now situation. Self-image problems are information gaps at the feeling level. "Thinking" about this can help you focus your attention, but to make changes or improvements, you have to be in touch with yourself on this emotional level.

That's what this chapter is about—exchanging information with your self at that basic feeling level. You will be able to give yourself useful information based on reality—a reality that gives you a reflection that is neither too big nor too small—rather, an accurate one. This chapter will also help you begin focusing on what you really want—what success in life means to you. This chapter is, in fact, about the "heart" of selling.

Ride 'Em Cowboy

When you were a little kid, unsure of who you were and so hopeful of who you would be, remember those daydreams centered around, "When I grow up, I'm going to be. . . ." Perhaps it was a cowboy, movie star, fireman, ballet dancer, but probably the same theme ran through all our earlier hopes for our futures. We were going to be great! Not just any old cowboy, but the one with golden spurs—the HERO! The best cowboy ever! The most we could squeeze out of cowboyhood.

Do you hear it? . . . the most, the best, the biggest, the greatest person we could be. Are you now the greatest, the biggest? What happened to that vision, the self-assuredness that we were going to be who we wanted to be?

Somewhere along the way we began hearing and heeding the voices of others. We decided they were right and we were wrong, or at least that our timing was off. Perhaps later we'd be "it". So, we hid our potential and ignored our daydreams. We—grew up.

And that was okay, because it allowed us to co-exist more comfortably and achieve goals more efficiently. But here we are: all grown and "mature," and still hoping for a cowboy's happiness—a happiness based certainly not on

1

the physical trappings of a cowboy's life, but, really, on the complete expression of our personality—the best cowboy, the best person, the BEST!

Guess what? That best person is still you. There is always time to be who you wanted to be deep down in your childhood's first awareness.

I want to take you through a series of discussions designed to help you understand and remove some of the barriers which experience has placed in front of the "essential" you. I want to discuss how your vision of yourself, your self-image, became changed and distorted, and how these changes resulted in a modification of your personality and an acceptance of someone other than who you really are.

In exchange, do me a favor—pass the word, share the understanding, help others appreciate their potential for greatness. We may learn to daydream again, and we may be wonderfully surprised to find that, this time around, we **are** the BEST!

Camera! Action! Roll 'Em!

Your life is what your thoughts make of it.
—Marcus Aurelius

There is a song in **"The Muppet Movie"** which contains a phrase I just love: "Life's like a movie, write your own ending; keep believing, keep pretending." This line carries so much of what I'm saying to you. Try to see your life as a movie with yourself as the script writer, the director, and the star. Only you can decide what type of movie this is going to be. It can be a tragedy—or a whopping success story. You alone can make that choice.

If your life has been scripted from a negative point of view with yourself as the "heavy" or maybe even the villain, incapable of being all you can, then take a fresh piece of paper—the new day—and begin writing your story from a different point of view. Script yourself as a capable, positive person who can set and achieve personal and professional goals.

In order to write this script for your movie, you must have objectives or goals which you want to achieve. Once you have set your goals you can work your way back to page one and begin scripting your story towards the accomplishment of these goals. Make your goals realistic so that the audience will believe your "story." If your script becomes unrealistic because it is chasing unrealistic goals, you will not believe it and your goals will not be achieved. Your script is really how you will manage yourself to accomplish your goals. (Chapter 3 will help you with the specific task of setting goals.)

If you can accept that you can write your own script, then you can accept and understand that you can change and rewrite your self-image. This is of central importance; you will live up—or down—to a good or bad self-image.

Weak sales associates do not pass on confidence to buyers or sellers. They fail and "live up" to what they "knew" all along.

Many of life's problems begin with your own self-evaluation. You are much like a computer who can be programmed for failure with a poor self-image—or for success through a positive script.

Don't be a person who carries with him his negative past; instead, throw it away. Do not let past experiences ruin your life. Why struggle along with the excess baggage of past frustrations? When you pack your suitcase for a trip, you only pack items which will make your trip smoother and more enjoyable; you leave the rest behind. The concept is the same as we prepare to "journey" into the future.

None of this is easy or foolproof. There are mistakes to be made while acting out your script. Too often people are not realistically aware of the difficulties involved with the achievement of goals. The experience can easily become negative when the first few failures occur. People begin to rationalize that they did not truly want to reach that goal anyway. They settle for failure because it is so accessible. The result is a lessening of self-image.

All experiences are either life-affirming or life-negating. Learn to structure more life-affirming situations and focus on their growth value to your self-image. The affirmation of life will increase your sense of value as a human being.

No one can make you feel inferior without your consent.
—Eleanor Roosevelt

Too often scripts are not followed because outside influences—family, friends, business associates—try to distract and change behavior to fit into their own scripts. These distractions are permitted because it is hard to break away from a weak self-image. But you can always choose to accept or reject this influence. You are in charge; you are the author.

You are an autonomous person, self-governing. Autonomy is the key to living your script as you wrote it. Others will try to dissuade you, but you can resist by choosing to accept responsibility for your own life. Your being can be no more than what you make it. Others cannot "make" you love or succeed; conversely, no one else can "make" you hate or fail. That right of choice is yours alone.

This is not just a case of "accentuate the positive"; it goes one giant step further than mere positive thinking. Positive scripting calls for action. It is the positive doing that creates the positive being. Just sitting around thinking good thoughts will not make them happen. Think . . . then act. Write your script . . . then take the stage . . . and star! As you learn to be the person you script, imagine yourself in this personality in much the same way an actor imagines himself in a role. Bring yourself to life by believing in yourself.

Just Who Do You Think You Are, Anyway?

To a large extent, you are your conception, your idea of yourself. You project this self image through attitudes towards events, feelings about people, expectations for the future, reactions to the past. Self-image reflects who you think you are . . . and what you think of yourself. This image colors and controls so much of what you think and do. It is rooted in the past, evolving in the present and determining the future.

Let's simplify:

Experiences determine self-image.

Self-image determines attitudes.

Attitudes determine behavior.

Behavior determines results.

Experiences, all those many contacts with life—some forgotten, many remembered, painful, joyous, significant, meaningless, negative or positive—all past events have shaped the person you are today. Experiences have molded your self-image which expresses itself through certain attitudes, behaviors and habits.

The concept of a self-image explains why some people are exhilarated and some defeated by a similar event. Your self-image is an important factor in whether you laugh or cry, feel threatened or secure, stop or go.

Unfortunately, most people live today with poor self-images. Their esteem and feelings of personal well-being have been tattered and fragmented by parents, teachers, and friends—also acting through poor self-images. Instead of emphasizing the good in an event: "Great! You got 99 right!"—Life's experiences often focus on the negative: "Oh! You missed one!"

It is sad that most of us face one of life's greatest challenges, the development of self, both ours and our children's, with far less preparation and training than is necessary. Most schools prepare us to use mathematics, English, and science, but not to use our own personal potential, nor to develop our own personal self.

But cheer up! Your self-image may have its basis in the past, but it has its evolution and development in the present. And the present is full of the possibility for growth and change. Previous experiences do not pre-determine future experiences. You have a powerful tool with which to influence your life—personal choice. You can accept responsibility for and take control of your self-image. Personal choice gives the freedom to discard what is negative within yourself and choose that which is positive and life-affirming.

So ask yourself who you think you are. See if there is much variance between who you are and who you want to be. Understand that the potential personality is possible. Who do you think you are, anyway? Wouldn't it be great to answer, "I am who I always wanted to be!"

Will the Real "You" Please Stand Up!

Remember those circus or carnival mirrors designed to distort your reflection as you pass by them? It's fun to see yourself change from "Wilt the Stilt" to "Two-Ton Baker" and everyone in between. And you always walk away laughing because you know that's not how you really look. The way you understand your inner self is oftentimes just as distorted and unstable as if it, too, were viewed through carnival mirrors. Only in this case the mirrors are those created by other people as they project their reflections of you.

Social psychologists agree that self-image is a combination of three perceptions:

(1) the person others see,

(2) the person you see, and

(3) the person you really are.

This third person, this one that must grapple with the realities of situations, is a combination of the first two perceptions. Others see and judge you by your actions; you see and judge yourself through your feelings. The result: a combination personality based largely on partial and distorted information. As you laughed at the person in the carnival mirror, so you must develop the ability to "laugh away" a distorted self-image which is harmful to your sense of well-being and not really representative of the "real" you.

An essential step in elevating your sense of personal worth is to accept your uniqueness as a person and to understand the specialness you hold because you are one of a kind. Why live through a negative self-value—a distorted image—which is as unreal as the reflections in the mirror? Why let others judge and define your worth? What value is there in evaluating yourself solely by how you feel and ignoring what you do and accomplish? You are capable of positive actions, so why let your feelings of inadequacy mar the fact of your outward success. You are a unique person capable of personal growth and accomplishment. This is the reality; this should be the cornerstone of your personal identity.

When you allow someone else to define your personality you will often have the tendency to sell yourself short. Remember, your negative self was developed in the first place because you allowed parents and teachers to instill in you their deflated version of your worth. Do not accept these negative feelings as reflections of your inadequacy. Do not believe someone else's limited vision of yourself. Just being a functioning human being is (or has) potential for greatness and brings with it a possibility for a greater future. Learn to stop focusing on weakness; instead, highlight your strengths, for it is only through strength that an improved self-image can develop. People do many things right in a day's time but somehow manage to remember mainly their mistakes. Then they reinforce these mistakes and exaggerate their importance when asked, "How was your day?" Learn to develop a response of positiveness to this question; learn to remind yourself of the good you performed that day. Accentuating your worth will put the day's frustations into proper perspective. Why waste time adding to a distorted and unreal self-image? If you measure yourself against others and your view of their accomplishments, you will also foster an unreal image of yourself. Certainly, some people may be smarter, stronger, faster, or better looking than you, but that fact makes you neither inferior nor superior. You are apart from others in your uniqueness and personal autonomy. You are also like others in that all people have strengths and weaknesses. It is unrealistic and unfair to compare their strengths with your weaknesses. Learn from others when you can, but resist the temptation to emulate someone whom you label as "better" than you are. Use external experiences for "research material" as you develop the personal greatness within yourself. Remember, you are your own "best" person. You are the person you must live up to.

> *Argue for your limitations and you get to keep them.*
> —Richard Bach

As you begin to recognize the distortions marring your self-image, you may discover that expectations are a major source of this distortion. Expectations, whether those perceived as coming from others or those you direct towards others, have an inordinate ability to influence and determine actions and responses. How can a person win who has been preconditioned to expect failure? Such negative expectations can so distort self-image as to place you in the position of "victim"— "Everything bad always happens to me!" The trick is to sort out the realistic and relative expectations you have for yourself and "laugh off" those which may be overly influential and are inhibiting your more natural responses.

Looking Clearly at Others

Just as your self image is distorted through the eyes of others, so your perception of others can likewise be misdirected. Expectations based on false information can only create more confusion. Learn to act from a positive point of view rather than from a source of potentially false and unrealistic perceptions.

Autonomy

Another important factor in how you see yourself is your autonomy, your ability to exist and feel good about yourself independent of your associations with others. An autonomous individual does not have the constant need to draw his self-esteem from others; he does not have to be around others in order to feel comfortable with himself. In fact, if you do not like being alone and are not able to feel good about yourself when alone, this may be a valuable clue to your negative self-image. If you want to spend time with someone you like, you must like yourself to enjoy time spent alone. Experience shows that one reason people do not like to be alone is because they do not know what to do or how to entertain themselves. Obvious, accessible pastimes—stimulating reading, creating with one's hands, developing a little-used talent, expanding on a passing interest—all will fill your "alone time" with good thoughts and feelings about yourself. This, in turn will enhance your self-image and make you more interesting to yourself. The most trustful, loyal, and interesting friend you have is always within you. If you have gotten "out of touch," rekindle the relationship. The growth and pleasure you experience will be well worth the effort.

Reflections of Your Reality

How you see yourself is all important. You act in accordance with the truth as you see it. But this truth can be distorted quite easily because of the role the subconscious plays in filtering and interpreting external experiences. An interesting example of the power of the subconscious is hypnosis. I have seen a hypnotist convince people they are unable to pick up a book because their subconscious reality had been so altered that they understood the weight of the book to be beyond their lifting capabilities. People often act, not because of reality, but because of their perception of it.

If you understand yourself to be a positive, effective person, you will make your reality agree. You will interpret external situations from a position of positiveness and will act accordingly. If, for example, you see yourself as a weak prospector, you will unconsciously gear your actions towards avoidance of prospecting, thus reinforcing your version of yourself as a weak prospector. "I never was any good at that!" But the same holds true if you understand yourself to be capable of effective prospecting; you will channel your energies into this activity, interpret situations on the basis of your positive feelings, and see success as reinforcement of your self-image.

If you feed negative thoughts into your subconscious, do not be surprised when you end up with a sour attitude. Learn to dine on positive thoughts and treat your subconscious, the source of your self-image, to a banquet of life-affirming feelings. Your version of reality will change and your ability to move forward may likewise surprise you. Take responsibility for the menu being served; choose only main courses, rich with the flavor of life and the spice of challenge. Allow your self-image to become satisfied with self-enjoyment.

Believe in yourself! If you don't, who will? It is really quite simple. Believing in yourself means following your personal script so the person you think you are is in control. It means allowing others to understand who you really are. It means doing away with the distortions and expectations you have learned to accept as a kind of self-protective covering, hiding the "real" you.

Hold Out Your Mirror to Others

It is possible to cause others to see who you know yourself to be through the power of a positive self-image. You can go beyond personal limitations when you refuse to accept them as limitations. Here's what I mean:

For as long as people thought about such things, it was believed that "man" could not run a mile in less than four minutes. The reality was that a sub-4-minute mile was impossible. Then May 6, 1954, Dr. Roger Bannister of Oxford, with a different vision of reality, ran a mile in 3 minutes 59.4 seconds. "Reality" had changed. During the next four years alone, the sub-4-minute mile was run forty-three times. But the real point of this story is the power of Roger Bannister's self-image. As a child he was told that he would never walk again. Who he was—a person who could not walk—did not change who he thought he was. Instead, his self-image as an achiever changed reality.

Thomas Edison, another reality changer, was a poor student as a child, but had unlimited belief in himself. In fact, his strong self-image enabled him to fail over 8,000 times in his effort to "light the world."

Chapter 2

Communications

One thing you can count on in Real Estate Sales—sooner or later you have to knock on the door.

Real estate is one-on-one communications day in and day out. It's truly the people business. And that's probably at least part of the reason why you're in the business—you like people.

But what does it take to actually go up to that door and knock? First, it takes a well planned rejection-free strategy, carefully structured and defined. More than that, you need a positive self-image, a realistic idea of who you are; you need clearly defined goals so you know *why* you're making this call and when and how long it will take; and you need communication skills, the ability to develop rapport, to realistically evaluate what others needs are, and to share useful information with them. You need to "hear" them and have them "hear" you.

So there's good reason for pause before knocking on that door; there is much intellectual and emotional energy going into that call.

This chapter on Communications presents those skills you need to "tune-in" to both the other person and yourself. You'll learn some easily accessible techniques for cutting through the screens and blocks in your interaction and getting to the heart of the matter. Remember, real estate sales are based on emotion—the other party's feelings about a home. If you haven't created an atmosphere where those feelings can come out, and haven't probed to uncover those feelings and the needs related to them, you probably won't make the sale.

The Problem of Communications

To put effective communication skills in perspective, you need to know or be reminded of the limits of communication:

WE ARE NEVER ABLE TO TOTALLY COMMUNICATE EXACTLY WHAT WE THINK AND FEEL WITH AN-OTHER PARTY—BECAUSE THEY CAN NEVER TO-TALLY UNDERSTAND US OR OUR FRAME OF REFERENCE.

We never know exactly how another person interprets what we say. That other party brings to an interaction all their past—what their parents, friends, spouses, brokers, and managers have said. This colors how they hear what you are saying. And you bring to the interaction the same kaleidoscope of influences and inferences, very few of which absolutely connect with the other party's experiences. In a way it's quite incredible that we can talk to each other at all. For example: if someone says "blue"—you might conjure up an image of royal blue; someone else—navy blue; someone else—a pastel blue. They're all blue, but all quite different. So there are inevitable limitations to any interaction. However, your goal is to make the interaction as clearly meaningful to both parties as possible. The following explanations will help you reach that goal.

The Impact Values within Communication

Effective communicating is a learned skill. Unfortunately, our instinct is to assume that people understand us; we have only to open our mouths and we will be both listened to and understood. This is likely a natural instinct, based on times that were simpler and more defined by clans or small groupings of people. Certainly it is not true of today. It is absolutely not true of anyone in sales. You meet such a variety of people that there are few assumptions you can realistically make. This challenges you, for the sake of survival, to learn good communication skills. You probably already have some good communication skills so the following information will serve to help you hone those skills and make them more useful.

Impact Value 1: Listening for Intonation

Words carry only 5 percent of the impact value of any interaction; vocal intonations carry 30 percent of the impact value. This reinforces the old statement that it is not as important what you say but how you say it. We can remember situations where we have said the same words to one person that we have said to other people and yet it has not had the same impact. This could happen while qualifying buyers. For example: you may have been in a situation where you ask them how many bedrooms they want and receive a hesitating or questionable four. You may have written down, on the qualifying sheet, that they are looking for four bedrooms. Yet, had you been able to read their vocal intonations and realize that they were questioning the four bedrooms, you could have clarified what they wanted—to make sure you had accurate information about their needs. Unfortunately, what happens too often in these circumstances is that you write down four on the qualifying sheet, then two weeks later find out that these people bought another house, through another agent, that only has three bedrooms. You then hear statements like, "buyers are liars." In reality, it is just a problem in communication. Had the sales associate pursued the discussion and read the vocal intonations, he could have questioned further to find out that maybe it was a case of they only needed three bedrooms but they needed another area for a workroom. This occurs in many areas of qualifying, not only with buyers but also with sellers.

Impact Value 2: Body Language

A powerful aspect of communications is body language. This has the greatest impact of all—45 percent, an even greater impact than the words we use or even the vocal intonations. While there are numerous books on the subject such as "How to read a person like a book" and "Body language," they quite unfortunately encourage us to develop our ability to read body language rather than to project it. That's a problem because it's the *projection* of our body language that is important in establishing rapport and trust with our clients or prospects. For example, if you are on a listing presentation and talk openly about your concern for their well being, yet your body language is defensive, or your eyes lack interest, you are probably negating everything you say.

A body language "rule of thumb" includes maintaining good eye contact, open body posture with arms and legs uncrossed, and leaning slightly forward with a pleasant smiling appearance. This is not to minimize the benefit of understanding or reading the other person's body language; however, your first concern should be to provide, through your positioning and eye contact, a comfortable atmosphere.

Some clues for what to watch for in the other party are:

- Eyes squinting—often means they don't understand what you are saying (check this out—ask if they have any questions or say, "You look like you have a question");
- Eyes drifting—you have probably lost their attention (move the discussion to another area or pick up the pace);
- Constant movement—they could be uncomfortable with the topic or time.

The point in watching body language—yours and the other parties'—is to watch for everything that words are not saying. Not ignoring the words, but checking to see what matches with the body language and what doesn't. Use this information to modify and clarify your interactions.

Impact Value 3: Environment

Any disruption in the environment where you are meeting has a 5 percent negative impact value. This means you have a greater chance of not succeeding in that interaction than if there are no disruptions. Therefore, it's necessary to do everything you possibly can to minimize disruptions. Try to control the setting so there are the least distractions possible. Choose to sit in a dining room rather than a living room or den where there might be a television or children playing.

Impact Value 4: Interruptions

Interruptions, such as children, are at times unavoidable. However, they do have a 40 percent negative impact value within your interaction. While some sales associates bring coloring books or other portable toys, the important point is not to interfere with other people's children. Don't correct them—you risk antagonizing the parents. At worst, it's a "grin and bear it" situation.

Impact Value 5: Proximity

Proximity is an issue that has a 5 percent impact value and is important to controlling a comfortable environment.

Proximity simply means the distance between the sender and receiver. Different people are comfortable in different spaces or with different space between sender and receiver.

Some people do not like to get as close to the other person as others. A guideline to follow is to be just over one arm's length away from the other person.

For your sake, you want to be sure to be sitting so that you can see the other party. (If there are two people, make sure you can have eye contact with both.)

The Parties Involved

There are two parties that make up any interaction: the sender and the receiver. Either party can be one or many people (i.e. a sales associate and a buyer, or a jazz trio and an audience).

What are the Components of Effective Communication?

An effective interaction includes the following:

A. Attention

The receiver must focus his *attention* on the sender. This doesn't mean eyes glued on the sender, but the basic focus must be on the eyes and face. *Attention* should also be the main focus of the sender. The sender must be looking at the receiver to maximize the level of communication.

B. Duplication

The receiver must have the ability to *duplicate* what is being communicated by the sender. When we talk about duplication we talk about xeroxing in our minds exactly what the sender is trying to say to us. We are talking not only about duplicating the words that they have said, but also duplicating the feelings which they have tried to pass on to us through their vocal intonations and body language.

C. Understanding

The receiver must be able to understand what the sender is trying to communicate. If, as the receiver, you are unable to understand, ask questions. In a selling situation it is especially important to ask questions of the sender. It may be the sender's obligation or responsibility to ask the receiver for confirmation as to whether they understand. Or the sender may ask for feedback on what has been discussed—"do you understand what I mean by? . . ."—this lets you know if understanding has been achieved.

D. Acknowledgement

Acknowledgement means that either the sender or receiver lets the other person know that he has heard what was said. A good way to explain acknowledgement is to show what happens when the receiver does not acknowledge that they have heard you.

An example occurred when I was recently flying back from a seminar. Hoping to get some rest, I asked the flight attendant, who was standing next to me, for a pillow. She reached up and opened the compartment above my seat. Not realizing that she had heard me, I repeated the question, "May I please have a pillow?" She looked down at me and said, "I heard you and I'm checking." Because she had not acknowledged my communication, I didn't realize that she had heard me and was responding by checking.

Be very aware of this need for acknowledgement when working with both buyers and sellers. Communicate acknowledgement through statements such as "I see," "I understand how you feel," "I appreciate your concern for that," or "that's a very important point."

Summary

In any interaction there are senders and receivers. An effective communication process includes these activities: attention, duplication, understanding, and acknowledgement. These activities are each a skill you need to develop and practice to be an effective communicator.

Barriers to Communication

To effectively communicate with someone, you inevitably have to work through barriers. A barrier is anything that blocks communication—and as you can imagine, based on your understanding of communications, there can be many. But the common ones that are critical to your success as a communicator are:

A. Poor Self-Image

This is probably the greatest barrier for effective communication—on the part of either the sender or the receiver. Because of poor self-image, we may be unable to look another person in the eye or we may be unable to really listen to what it is they say. We are so hung up in what we are going to say, because of our insecurity, we are unable to let things flow. A poor self-image also forces us not to confront issues that may be of prime importance. We don't confront these often because of a lack of confidence in our ability to handle the problem or the concern. An inability to listen often stems from feeling like we've always got to be selling ourselves—again poor self-image.

A poor self-image many times will also force us to "mask" our communication. People have a tendency to believe that if they are totally open and honest they won't be liked. Their poor self-image makes them feel that people will only see undesirable qualities in them. Therefore, they mask and hide their true feelings and thoughts. This can "set the tone" for an interaction. The other party may well respond in kind, masking and hiding their true feelings and thoughts. Yet, this is devastating to a sales interaction where you *know* people buy on emotion. It's very important that they are open and honest so that you not only hear what they say but also have an understanding of how they feel.

B. Assuming That People Know What You Are Talking About

The second major barrier to effective communications is an unwarranted assumption that people know what you are talking about. This is a distinct danger in any business where there is a great deal of business jargon. The California Association of Realtors has a study showing that the public does not truly understand many of the words used in real estate. Of all the people they interviewed 61.1 percent did not know what the term "earnest money" meant, 36.4 percent did not know what "assumable" meant, and 38.9 percent did not know what a "listing" was. Yet, how many times have you heard a sales associate say, "We just got a great new listing that has an assumable mortgage, and you can get into it with very little earnest money"? The associate may think he has communicated effectively with these people and yet has not. The problem is compounded because often in situations like this, people will have a tendency not to question what was said, and just allow the associate to continue. They may even nod their heads rather than show their inadequacy or failure to understand what it was that we said. This is related, of course, to their self-image. People that have a weak self-image will not question a lot of things that we say even though they don't understand because they feel that it might show their ignorance.

Watch out for business jargon, and watch the body language of your listeners very carefully. Check out their understanding and explain in non-jargon what it is you have said if they haven't understood.

C. Breaks in Concentration

Sometimes in the midst of communication between two people, there is a break in concentration on the part of the receiver because of a misunderstood word. This break in the flow causes the receiver's mind to wander and is therefore a tremendous barrier to the interaction. Mental wandering also causes a break in the concentration and is a barrier to effective communication. While we can talk at approximately 150 words per minute, we actually think at a rate of about three to four times that amount, so it is very natural for the mind to wander in a conversation, but it also is dangerous because we lose our focus. Try to focus once again and duplicate what it is that the sender is trying to say to us.

D. External Distractions

Some common barriers to watch for (in addition to those discussed in the components of communication) are:

- A phone ringing in your office when trying to talk with a buyer or seller.
- Lack of interest on the part of the sender or receiver.

As you've probably seen and heard, sales associates with positive attitudes seem to be more successful. They not only have an interest in the people that they are dealing with but they also have an interest in their product. Realize that your interests are not necessarily going to be the same as the people with whom you are dealing. To find an area of interest, make sure the topic is applicable to their situation. Many times we can see whether there is any lack of interest or not through the body language of the receiver. Make sure you are committed to your work and your product—if you are not sincere, it shows and you're wasting your time.

E. Personal Crisis

It is very difficult to communicate with another person if there has been a personal crisis, such as an illness or injury, or personal relationship problems in the family—either theirs or yours. Take these factors into consideration when observing that someone has changed his way of thinking or maybe is irritable one day, while on other days seemingly willing to listen and communicate.

F. Poor Organization

Poor organization is another barrier to effective communication. This often results from a lack of proper intention on the part of the sender. If we are striving for effective communication, it is important that you organize your thoughts carefully, rather than ramble. If you move from one area to another sporadically or haphazardly, it is very difficult for the receiver to follow your message. Therefore it limits your communication. While in most sales situations we cannot predict everything that might happen, it is important that we have a planned presentation that takes your clients from point A to point B and on through point Z.

G. Lack of Product Knowledge

Did you ever try to sell something that you knew absolutely nothing about? If you have, then you can realize how lack of knowledge is another barrier to effective communication. The more knowledge you have, the more you are able to be flexible in meeting the needs of your clients. If you have a limited knowledge about your product, then you can only present it in a limited manner.

Lack of product knowledge also effects your ability to confront problems and issues that come up with buyers and sellers. If you don't know something, you will avoid confronting the problem.

H. Lack of Trust

If there is a lack of trust, the sender or the receiver will do more masking and will pay less attention to what is actually being said. This clearly inhibits any interaction.

I. Wishful Hearing

Speaking of thinking of what might be being said, a real danger is in the area of wishful hearing. You've heard about wishful thinking, well wishful hearing is quite similar. You hear what you want to hear rather than what the sender is actually trying to say. An example of this would be if you're working on a listing presentation and tell the seller that his home is worth somewhere between $75,000 and $80,000; what he or she primarily hears is the $80,000 figure. Be very careful that you don't mislead them accidentally because of wishful hearing. Wishful hearing usually occurs in two areas—price and time. If you give any indication that you can sell their home quickly, even if you use a lot of information to support the fact that you cannot control it, because of wishful hearing the sellers will expect you to sell it quickly. You have set their expectations—they did not hear the further explanation.

J. Appearance

Last on the list of barriers to effective communication, but by no means least, is appearance. The clothes you wear, the way that you groom yourself, the way that you walk, the way that you carry yourself, all these things make impressions upon the person with whom you're trying to communicate. If these impressions lead to a negative feeling on the part of the receiver, he is not going to listen as attentively and/or he is not going to trust the things that we say because of this break. Many times, people ask what is considered proper dress for people in a business situation. Although different areas have different standards, or different products have different standards for dress, in the real estate business you can never be out of place by dressing conservatively. Usually the best way to dress is with a dark blue or grey suit with a white shirt or blouse underneath and a tie or scarf to match.

An interesting study concerned a director of a consulting company who took two of his people with him to a Board of Director's meeting. In the first meeting, the man was dressed in a blue three-piece suit, white shirt and matching tie, the woman was dressed in a blue skirt with a blue jacket and a light colored blouse underneath. After the Board of Director's meeting the man in charge of the consulting firm said that from that point on the associates would be handling this client, if it was OK with the Board. Although his associates said absolutely nothing during the meeting, the Board voted almost unanimously to accept them.

The same two associates were taken to another Board of Director's meeting a couple of weeks later—this time dressed very casually. They both had on jeans and a sport shirt open at the collar. After the meeting, the director of the consulting firm presented the same statement: that his associates from this point on would be handling this account with their permission. This time the Board voted resoundingly against these two people. Again, the two associates had said absolutely nothing at the meeting.

Although we have a tendency to say people should judge us by what we are capable of doing rather than how we look or how we dress, in the real world this is not the case.

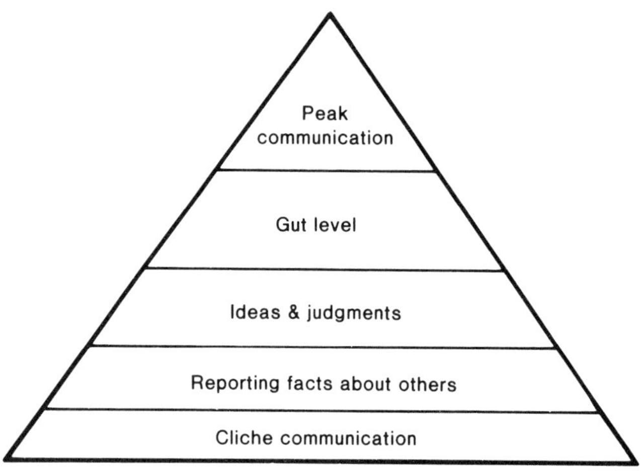

Levels of Communication

Because effective communication is, especially in today's world, an acquired and quite necessary skill—many people have taken the time to study and define it. Some of the research on Levels of Communication is very important to you, as a salesperson. It can help you be aware of and develop the various levels of communication you will need to find satisfaction in your work—and in your life. The sales field is the same as the field of life, meaning that if you are able to communicate with people in your everyday personal life and communicate effectively, you will also be able to communicate with people in a selling situation.

Keep in mind that communication occurs on many levels:

Level 1: Cliche Conversation

The first level is cliche conversation. This is what you will experience most often. This is the level of communication where people are just casually saying things like "how are you?" and "nice to see you" but are not really that concerned with the answers. In fact, if you are at the theatre or outside a seminar watching a group of three or four people, you will notice that one of them is usually talking about his or her favorite topic—himself, and the other two or three people are standing around kind of daydreaming and maybe halfheartedly listening, but mostly waiting to talk about their favorite topic—themselves.

Level 2: Reporting Facts about Others

The second level of communication is reporting the facts about others. This means simply that people are stating things such as "Did you see the game yesterday?" "Did you hear what Pam did?" or any type of gossip or reporting of facts.

Level 3: Ideas and Judgments

The third level of communication gets into the area that many people mask, due to a weak self-image. This is the level of ideas and judgments. When we start sharing our ideas and judgments we realize that it is a little risky— we let people know who we are. Once you start to share these ideas and judgments with others, they are going to either agree or disagree with them, and therefore may like you or not (especially if you do not have the same ideas and judgments). This is the reason most people like to stay within the first two levels of communication, simply because they are afraid they are not going to be liked. For you to communicate effectively with other people, you need to know who they are. This also means you have to share with them who you are, which includes sharing your ideas and judgments.

Level 4: Gut Level

The fourth level of communication is Gut Level communication. After you have communicated with people at a cliche level, and have also reported certain facts to them and expressed some ideas and judgments, you're now ready to share your emotions and feelings with these people. An example of this might be a statement such as "I think you are bright and being with you is a pleasure," which is a statement of ideas and judgments followed by how that makes you feel. If you are willing to share your feelings with others, they are more willing to share their feelings with you. Again, re-emphasizing the point that people buy on emotions which are simply feelings. Therefore, in order to get them to share their feelings and emotions with us, we have to share ours with them.

Level 5: Peak Communication

The fifth level of communication is peak communication and it is extremely difficult. This is the area where you must have absolute openness and honesty. This is not necessarily an area you get into with clients or prospects, but it is definitely a level of communication that we should hope to reach with the people who are closest to us. Once you start communicating on a peak level, the people begin to understand who you truly are. You do not have any masks, you admit there are some flaws, you are willing to share those flaws with the people that you love, and you are not ashamed to admit them.

Probably one of the biggest personal relationship problems is in this area of communications. What happens frequently in the courting or dating process is that both the man and the woman only show their good side; they have a tendency to hide their idiosyncracies or the negative aspects of their personalities. What happens then, after a dating process that lacked peak communication, is a marriage with all the problems that could have been eliminated or at least been understood had there been peak communication. Too many husbands and wives say how much their spouse has changed since they were married. In reality that spouse did not change, he or she just was being who he always was; but for whatever reason his/her negative side was not shown during the courting process.

Rules for Gut and Peak Communication

If you intend to participate in either gut level or peak communication, there are certain rules to follow:

1. *Never imply a judgment of the other when they open up to us.* When one party, the sender, makes a statement about how they feel, very openly and honestly, and the receiver makes a judgment—maybe critical of the sender—peak communication is inhibited. Your opportunity for very real communication is cancelled out.

2. *Realize that emotions are not moral, that emotions just are.* For example, in the area of sexual feelings—it is very normal for a man or a woman to have feelings or emotions toward someone other than their spouse, or somebody with whom they are having a close personal relationship. Having these feelings does not make them a bad person, but many times they are inhibited in talking about them with the people closest to them, because they feel that they will be judged and considered immoral. Having these feelings does not mean we are going to act on them—it only means we have them.

3. *Feelings and emotions must be integrated with the intellect and will.* This means that after having these feelings or emotions you still can think them through and think of what is the best course of action to take.

It is more important to have people be truthful than to mask their feelings and ideas. Yet, how many times have you felt that you don't want to be truthful with someone else for fear of hurting them. It would be much better for people to be open, honest, and truthful, so that you could deal with them and the world as it really is rather than as one might irrationally wish it were.

Because man is a social being, the ability to communicate is at the heart of our feelings of self-esteem and well-being. All levels of communication are good. They provide an opportunity for us to reach out and share with someone. Attaining certain levels of communication are particularly gratifying and significant in our lives. However, the level of communication varies in appropriateness according to the circumstances you are in. Versatility in communicating at various levels according to circumstances is a great asset to your life and sales career.

Chapter 3

Goals and Time Management

Have you ever met someone, or heard of someone, who has everything—all the necessities for a comfortable life and more? Yet, you have the feeling that they are like a child who gets a shiny new bike but never learns or even tries to ride it. While it's the unlikely child that this would happen to, unfortunately there are many adults in this world who, like the child with a new bike, have never quite learned to enjoy what they have, who they are, or simply the day in which they are living. This is an enormous loss—but one that can be changed.

In this chapter you'll have the opportunity to put the wishes, dreams, and hopes you uncovered or discovered in Chapter 1 into a concrete plan based on your goals and priorities; and you'll be able to work into a schedule that allows you the most opportunity to enjoy yourself, your life, and each day—while working towards meaningful goals.

The following ideas will show you how to grab hold of your time and focus it on your goals. It is a method of organizing and managing your life.

Taking Control of Your Life and Time

If you could control time—you probably would.

You would stretch, bend, fold, spindle and in every way lengthen or shorten or change the hours to fit your needs. Of course, the passage of time itself cannot be controlled like the hands of a clock, but, in a way, you can manage time—by managing yourself and your use of time. The hours, days, and weeks of your life can be managed to allow you to use them as you wish. You can schedule more time for what is most important to you and leave enough time for other things that need to be done, but which may not have the same gut level priority.

Perhaps you are weary of the feeling that time is passing you by and, not only do you not know "where the time went," you still find yourself no closer to your goals. If you can check off a list of "To Do's" accomplished for the day, why don't you feel you are moving ahead? Where are you going, anyway? And why not fast enough?

There are many occasions when we all feel this way, especially when events in our lives raise their red banners announcing that time is passing: the baby of the family starts school or graduates; another Happy New Year comes and goes; a friend retires and you start to check your own retirement date; or maybe it's the beginning of another fiscal year when you realize it is time to grow—but again you find you are not sure how or in what direction.

Setting Goals—with the Heart

Start with desire. The dictionary defines desire as a longing, craving or yearning for something near at hand, or near in thought, and viewed as attainable. We speak of our appetite or passion to possess an object or a state of being. On this level desire seems almost physical, a very real feeling that we must *do something* to attain the object of our desire. Translate this physical yearning for an object to the attainment of a specific goal and you will see the importance of your desire as a motivating source.

When you plan to make prospecting contacts, do you approach the task as an uncomfortable but necessary evil, something you know to be important to your success, but which certainly fails to "turn you on"?

What would it take to add "desire" to your attitude, the kind of desire that really motivates you . . . a "desire" that helps you make a clear connection between your performance and goal attainment. And that goal fills you with such longing that you simply *must* have it. This kind of desire is like a flame; it can be intensified until it directs you to the things you want as well as directing you to be the person you want to be.

This flame of burning desire does not operate on the thinking, rational level, but is part of the emotional feeling self—the heart. It involves your whole being as a motivational source because it puts you directly in touch with your longings and cravings. If you first think with the head instead of feeling with the heart you risk altering your desires as they are filtered through the influences of peer pressure, expectations, various rationalizations, and perceived limitations. What comes out then bears little resemblance to what the heart originally felt and, there is little chance of fueling that flame which probably no longer exists. Don't let this happen to you. Identify that flame—and whatever ignites it and turns it up; let yourself feel the power of desire to motivate and move you.

Feelings are an important part of all you do. (Before you can dance you must sense the beat of the music.) You know how good you will feel when you finally finish cleaning the garage and can actually find something again. It was this feeling of satisfaction which motivated you towards the garage in the first place. For much the same reason you plan a large dinner party because you enjoy the compliments garnered from appreciative guests. Rarely does the doing of a task itself provide the full satisfaction; anticipation of the end rewards provides the motivational source. And the most rewarding activities are those which, in some way, make you feel good about yourself by directly responding to a basic desire.

In your professional life as a real estate agent, you work with people who desire to buy a home. Their motivation for buying the home may involve a reward for success in their professional lives. Yet, what is your motivation for helping them achieve their goal? Is it becoming personally involved with them and really caring to be a part of their endeavor? Or are you working, not for them, but for the commission due you for success? Aren't you really working hardest for the person who means the most to you—yourself?

Choosing commission over caring does not mean you *don't* care about your clients and their goals, only that you care about yourself and your goals. Think about it: you hardly know these people and, after this transaction is completed, will see them only rarely in the future. To what extent can you truly care about them on such a short-term basis? But you know yourself intimately and will continue to care about your happiness long after these people are replaced by others and other goals. You are the continuum throughout your experiences. Who but you holds the spark that lights the flame that motivates you to get the job done?

"Getting the job done" means you will earn a good commission. Now translate "commission" into feeling good about yourself and increasing your self-esteem. This may mean your selection as salesperson of the month; your family's encouragement and applause; or peer recognition that you are someone who knows what needs to be done. When commission means more money for a new car, the purchase of a "too-expensive" suit or a "once in a lifetime" vacation that you take every year—or whatever you want and however you want to feel—then it has the power to motivate. But first you must feel what you want and who you want to be. Goal setting is the way these feelings become tangible realities.

Life Is More Than a Trip to the Moon

Some friends of mine are taking a long-anticipated and hard-earned trip to Hawaii. They have purchased their tickets, confirmed their rooms, and scheduled their island tours. This weekend they plan to shop for new bathing suits and sportswear. They have arranged for someone to check the house and water the plants during their absence. They have reserved kennel space for their two cats. The checklist of last minute details is growing daily in their efforts to do everything they can to insure a great trip to the islands. They have worked hard and plan to enjoy themselves to the fullest.

As they return from this dream trip, reminiscing over their pictures and memories, they will reenter the normal flow of their lives, continuing on their daily journey. However, there is one significant difference: the vacation was planned and prepared for—their daily life is not. They have no plans, no checklists, no goals to insure that this most important trip, their lives, is also great. They just "go," stopping along the way for refreshments and resuming when they build up steam.

Life is a trip from who we are to who we want to be. We work hard at it and want to be able to enjoy it as a reward for our efforts. Why, then, do we not take the time to make some plans: decide what our destination is and develop a checklist to insure we reach this goal.

Statistics are sometimes helpful. A study conducted with recent Harvard graduates revealed that 83 percent had no goals for their future; 14 percent had goals for the coming year; and 3 percent had specific goals (in writing) outlining their plan on a one year and five year basis. The results were (measured a few years later):

The 14 percent with goals were <u>earning three times as much</u> as those who had no defined goals.

The 3 percent with specific goals in writing were <u>earning ten times more</u> than most of the graduates who had no goals.

Why? Because clearly defined and understood goal setting provides a blueprint for action and a direction for achievement. Written goals are a tangible, concrete admission to ourselves of what we want to be and how we will get there. It gives the future a foothold in the present. Real goals become exciting and excitement ignites the flame and sets it blazing. If you have a clear idea or vision of what you want in life, you can channel your energies towards that goal; without a goal or vision, you go through life feeling puzzled as to why you are doing something or where you are going.

Before you can establish a goal, you have to get to the source of what is exciting to you. You have a whole world of possibilities. The question is: which ones will turn up your flame; which ones will make you so happy, once attained, that you are willing to plan and work hard towards their achievement? What is really important to you?

The First Step

Contrary to what many people think, the first step in goal setting is *not* pinpointing and enumerating your goals. Before you begin to think about goals, you must back up a square and first think about what really matters to you in your personal and professional life. Do you know what is important in your life and can you rate these items by relative priority? Once you have identified what is really important to you, you can begin to establish goals which will have meaning because they are a means to an end. The result is not just the accomplishment of a specific goal but rather the development of a life in which you will be doing the things *you* want to do because they are important to *you*. TAKE A MINUTE NOW TO TRY THE SELF-EXERCISE ON PAGE 82.

Now review the list of *life goal categories,* below, *in terms of your personal and professional life, desires, and needs.* Arrange and rearrange these items until you are able to prioritize each according to their value to you. Pay no attention to what you think *should* be important. Eliminate the pressures of society, peers, or family, whose ideas may radically differ from your own. As you think about this list, remember you are searching for the spark that will light the flame. What really turns you on—makes you say "Yes, I want to do that?" Uncover motivations which may be hidden from even yourself. Be honest in your evaluation of your true desires.

You may be tempted to prioritize your list on the basis of past learning (your "head" may say): "*logically,* love and family *should* be first." But if you find yourself ruled by your head, your list will not reflect *your* true desires as much as it will reflect the wants and needs of others around you. This is the time to let your feelings loose and identify what's really important to you.

Life Goal Categories

Service to Others	Independence
Power	Recognition/Fame
Religion	Health
Morality	Love/Family
Money/Wealth	Aesthetics/Art
Challenging Work	Fun/Recreation
Security	

After you have worked with this list and examined where you are and where you want to be, you will find that important items tend to remain fairly constant in your life. *What changes is how you feel about these things in relation to how closely and actively you are pursuing them.* For example: Independence may have always been important to you, but now you realize anew how essential it is to your feelings of well-being. The more successful you become, the more your self-esteem is based on *your* perceptions and feelings.

Note: You may find it difficult to assign different values to several categories which seem of equal value to you. That's okay; the primary exercise is to examine your feelings about your priorities.

Once you sort out your desires and clearly *feel* where your priorities lie, you can begin to set goals to bring you closer to what you want in life. You can stop living from minute to minute; you can take control of your life; you can manage that most precious commodity—your time.

Before going any further, complete the self-exercise on page 84.

First Down and Goal to Go

Now that you have honestly evaluated your priorities and determined what parts of your life you are truly interested in developing, you have taken the first step in living for the most important person in your life—yourself.

25

You will find it much easier to set goals that excite you when you can see how they will benefit you directly. Your goals will evolve naturally from your prioritized desires and you will be able to focus directly on these desires as the source of your flame, your motivation.

The emphasis when determining priorities and establishing goals must always be on self. Since no one lives in a vacuum and people generally have a need for relationships and personal interactions, it is important to understand that goal setting for self is a cornerstone for growing, vital, and rewarding relationships with other people.

The key to satisfactory relationships is continuity of interests resulting in shared experiences. This is true of casual friendships and long-term commitments as well. The more you have in common with another—the more shared priorities and goals that exist—the more the friendship develops and the more meaningful the union becomes. A positive environment develops when two people are able to share priorities and goals, with neither person depending on the other as their main source of satisfaction. Instead, both parties, independently or mutually, establish a program or life style to insure goal attainment, and both parties share the activities and experiences they have in common. Attaining this, they will have found a "soul-mate"—another person whose desires kindle a similar flame.

Begin now to think of what you need to accomplish in a year's time to bring your activities in line with your prioritized values. Do not evaluate or reject thoughts as they come. Just open up to things you would like to do, events you want to be a part of, where you would like to be next year. Rewrite parts or all of your life. Try scripting more exciting activities and more rewarding accomplishments. Let your feelings flow. Turn off the influence of your head which can be inhibiting and stifling. Open your heart and see what burns brightest within.

Goals—Making Them Your Own

On the next few pages are descriptions of the components of meaningful goals. Read through these before finalizing your thoughts and feelings about your own goals. Use them to help you shape and mold your thoughts so that you can finally write them down.

Components of Meaningful Goals

1. Goals Should Be Stimulating but Attainable

We were all created equal but our own special set of experiences, preferences, and talents have shaped up differently so that, today, we each have a unique set of possibilities. Take these capabilities and develop them to their maximum potential. Do not wait to be "discovered" by someone else who will direct your talents. Trust in yourself enough to make your own discoveries and guide your own life. Just be realistic. Make sure your skills match your aspirations. If you love classical music, setting a goal to perform in an opera company may be foolish if you can't carry a tune. But you may have the organizational skills to be a producer of operas or a stage manager. So you set that as your goal and develop a program of activities that will help you achieve this goal. If this realistic prospect stirs your flame, then you will be far more motivated than if you choose a singing career which is beyond your talents.

Setting unattainable goals is often a cop-out for nonachievement and results in a life based on "someday I'm going to be. . . ." These goals always wait for that elusive "tomorrow" to come to fruition. Set your goals in the present tense and plan for achievement in the reality of today. Visualize how you will feel as you approach accomplishment of your goals. When this vision stirs you to action, you will know you are on the right track.

2. Goals Must Be Set by You

Not as obvious as it sounds. Most people write their life scripts according to the expectations of family, peers, or authority figures. These subtle but powerful influences mask and confuse the desires of the heart, resulting in a goal list full of "shoulds" instead of wants. Accepting the standards of others without questioning their relevance to your desires is no fun. It results in a life busy with pursuing shoulds and little time for wants. Share your goals with your boss and family; but first make sure they evolve from your own heart. The only way to turn up the flame is to be aware of your feelings.

Look forward to the day when someone says to you, "You seem to do everything you want to do." You know then you are in control of your life and able to identify the sources of your flame. Why would you choose to do anything but what you want to do? It is okay to be selfish when writing goals for your life. Whose life is it, anyway?

3. Aim for Growth, Not Perfection

By definition you are a perfect person in your uniqueness, singularity and autonomy. But there is no perfect state of being or accomplishing. Every act performed is only a shadow of an ideal state. So your goals should stress improvement in action rather than striving for an unattainable ideal. To only accept the perfect accomplishment is to doom yourself to failure resulting in a lessening of self-image and a retreat from striving. Each attainable goal accomplished results in growth—one step at a time on the ladder of achievement. Aim for a little bit of growth. Aim to be better today than yesterday.

4. Goals Should Be Personal as Well as Professional

Your life is part business and part personal. Be sure to include both aspects when considering your goals, for you are a whole person and do not exist at work independent of who you are at play. The goals for these different areas will vary, but not the priorities from which the goals evolve. The list of your priorities deals with all aspects of your personality and life; goals should be reflective of and responsive to the particular texture of your desires. It is impossible to compartmentalize your life and, in fact, unnecessary to even try.

5. Goals Must Be Well Defined

Write your goals so they are clearly defined and related to your priorities. If you have discovered health and a slimmer appearance is really important to you, do not stop at "I will lose twenty pounds." Continue with a specific "how to" plan: "In six months I will lose twenty pounds by joining the noon exercise class at the Y and by eliminating sweets and between-meal snacks from my diet." If you plan to be a million dollar salesperson, state this so that it relates to your true motivation—"I will strive for more recognition (or more money—or both) by becoming a million dollar salesperson." Be specific: list particular steps you are going to take to insure your success. Then break down this yearly goal into monthly and weekly checklists. Determine how many new contacts should be made each week, how frequently your territory should be farmed, how many listings and closings you will need each month in order to bring you to your goal at the year's end. Visualize what this accomplishment will mean in terms of increased prestige at home and work, what you can do with the increased income and how this will make you feel. The mere fact of being a million dollar producer, or of losing twenty pounds, will not, in itself, be sufficient reward. The flame will glow when you visualize what that good attainment means—perhaps admiring looks or better self-image, whatever is your true reward.

You must formulate clearly what your goals are and when you are going to accomplish them. Goals must be well defined so you will feel their importance to you as you work to achieve them.

6. Goals Must Be in Writing

When your goals are in writing, you know where you are in relation to where you want to be, and you have a means for reviewing your progress constantly. Remember: it is through the doing that the being evolves. You cannot become who you want to be without acting on it today. Having your goals in writing serves as a reminder—the tendency to lose track of priorities can be avoided. The flame needs the fuel of awareness to keep burning.

In the preliminary stage of listing goals, do not make any attempt to eliminate or evaluate the worthiness or even the appropriateness of wants as they occur to you. There is no penalty for not reaching all goals nor do all goals have to be significant or meaningful in the eyes of the world. Later we will discuss prioritizing goals in relation to what is really important and what will be helpful to your success.

7. Goals Must Be Reviewed Constantly

Remember you will need to have this written list of goals to constantly refer to. Creating this daily awareness of your priorities will give you control over the structure of your life. You will be able to relate your priorities to your daily or weekly self-management schedule, and you will be able to review them easily to make sure you are moving forward. This awareness and management plan will enable you to go to work with real purpose rather than going to work and waiting for something to happen to provide direction. Interruptions and requests to do things are probably fulfilling someone else's goals and, if you fail to control their influence, you will spend your time away from your own priorities. At times you may choose to be interrupted; the difference is your awareness that the "interruption" may be part of your goal plan.

If you don't know where you are going, it's easy to get careless with time, then find yourself mourning its passing. Sometimes, it seems far more comfortable to abandon the struggle for growth and relax in the short-term ease of non-accomplishment. Then again, you may be so busy accomplishing and doing, that you get off on a tangent and begin to devote too much time to only one component of what will make you happy. Your worklife may overpower your family life and distort the real balance between the two you have desired to maintain. A constant review of what is important to you helps you set daily priorities based on your goals and gives you control over your time. You are managing your time and yourself by knowing where you are in relation to who you want to be. Examine your goals habitually to keep your fingers on the pulse of your life's flow.

Setting Priorities on Your Priorities

Your goal list, once developed, must be based on significant wants in your life and, if you really open up your mind to dreams and wishes, will be quite long and, obviously, impossible to control and achieve in total. What is needed is some way to rank and distinguish your goals so your time will be well spent on accomplishment. Crucial to self-management is a believable, attainable, inspiring, flame-producing list of priorities. Goals become the impetus behind successful self-management for they provide motivation, a way of measuring progress made and a map for maintaining a true course. Organizing and setting priorities on these goals is as easy as A, B, C.

"A" Priorities are tasks which you *must* do because they are critical to successful goal performance in relation to who you want to be and where you want to go. These items are important and urgent and *must* be done *now,* not someday, later, or never. On a daily self-management list "A" Priorities must be done *today* because of their direct contribution to your success. Their importance is such that they cannot be delegated to anyone but yourself. They

tend to be risk-taking by definition and are usually difficult and sometimes even unpleasant. Their payoff, however, is worthwhile for the time and ego invested. Examples include: visiting For Sale By Owners, working in your farm area, contacting expired listings, prospecting for referrals, and showing properties.

"B" Priorities should be done today because they are critical to your successful performance but they *may* be temporarily postponed without directly reducing your effectiveness. They are important but not urgent. On a daily self-management plan they must be done, but as time permits. Come tomorrow you must re-evaluate and reset priorities on these items—the passage of time has a way of promoting "B" items to an "A" status. Caution: it is very tempting to place difficult items into "B" priorities as a way of putting off tackling unpleasant tasks. It may take some time before you really understand the significance of these categories and are able to honestly evaluate and faithfully follow-through on these priorities. Refer often to your list of goals to rekindle your flame and motivate you to action.

"C" Priorities are nice to do. Accomplishing these is desirable but not critical to successful performance and they are sometimes urgent but not important. On a daily self-management basis you may determine that, while this may be the only day you can do the task, if you do not do it, that is okay too. If "C" items never get done at all—that is still okay. Caution: you may want to promote "C" into "A" items because of their comfort and ease and forget that they need not be completed. Be aware of the tendency to rationalize their importance, thus wasting "A" time on "C" items.

It takes some practice to learn to correctly rank goals by their A, B, or C value on the basis of what you—and not other people—think you should be doing. You will always be reminded of others' preferences. Your family members will be promoting their goals which may include "should do's" for you; management, as a part of their plan for success, will likewise have a list you "should" adopt as your own. Listen and evaluate those suggestions to see where they fit into *your* scheme of priorities and goals. Be open to these suggestions as a means for further stimulation and direction towards your goals. Just be aware that the final criterion for planning what you will be doing with your time is their relevance to your priorities and their ability to turn up your flame.

Remember: if you want to grow and fulfill your life script you must be willing to tackle your "A" priorities. You must be willing to chance the discomfort of risk-taking and the possibility of failure—to chance the possibility of success. The only way to move forward is through accomplishment of the "A" list of goals. *The fact that you may try and not succeed is not at all important.* The only thing that matters is the doing. If you try and fail you will remain where you are and nothing will be lost. But to try and then succeed—if only by a little bit—means forward advancement; you are closer to where you want to be!

Goals Are Wishes Coming True

You are now ready to actually list your goals, starting from today to one year from today. Use your earlier list of priorities as the source of your inspiration, remembering that goals get you to the point where you can accomplish what you know to be important in your life. At this point, concentrate on long-range goals and even include five-year goals as well as annual goals. Ramble as you go; include what *might* be important without qualifying real value or relevance. Reach out for some heretofore secret yearnings, something you have never thought seriously about because you never really took the time to map out a plan whereby you might accomplish the wish. Do not worry that your list may be getting too long and frightening in its demands. The next step is to set priorities.

When you have exhausted your "wish list" and dug deep for things you would like to do and be, start to evaluate your options by the "A-B-C" criteria, always using your list of important priorities as the standard for comparison. If health is very important to you and jogging two miles per day is a goal, then jogging will be an "A" priority. Continue through your list and measure each goal by how it will help you be who you want to be. Feel the effect of this measurement by feeling the intensity of the flame it stirs. Do not delegate a goal to the "B" or "C" category because you are afraid to acknowledge the commitment involved when assigning it as an "A" priority; remember, the goal will be approached day by day and never whole or in its entirety. Chips of accomplishment will be carved from the task, each one bringing you closer to attainment. Importance of the goal and time spent in working towards it are not related. You may spend more time at work-related goals, but health, at which considerably less time is spent, may still be an "A" priority. (However, be cautious not to build in too many changes at one time. Spread them out— try doing one at a time.)

Within these "A, B, C" categories, rank each goal numerically, resulting in an A1, A2, A3, B1, B2, B3, C1, C2, C3, etc., list. As with all these lists you are developing, feel free to alter and rearrange as much as necessary, as long as your heart is in control over the practicality or censoring influence of the head. Your final list will emerge as a fairly true reflection of who you want to be and how you plan to get there if you heed your heart.

Goal setting is not a one-shot, isolated event but should be viewed as a continuum of activity towards a defined priority. You may want to organize your list on an annual, monthly, and weekly basis or by five years, one year, and monthly. Organize your list so you have continuity and a useful tool for daily planning.

Once you know what is important in your life and have ranked your list of goals to insure these important priorities will be achieved, you are ready for action. List what you are going to do in the next seven days to start accomplishing your goals. Be specific and define your activities exactly. This weekly plan will form the blueprint for daily action.

TRY THE SELF-EXERCISE ON PAGE 85.

Once a week make an appointment with the most important person you know, yourself. (You would not think of cancelling out on such an influential person.) For this meeting be prepared to discuss the topic: BECOMING WHO I WANT TO BE. First, review your goals and accomplishments for the preceding week. Evaluate what you did in terms of how much closer you are to your priorities. If you missed performing some goals, decide why:

1. Was it because you miscalculated the importance of a task—reevaluate it—is it truly an "A" priority? Or,

2. Did you just not complete an important "A" item and need to carry it over to your goal list for the coming week?

Give yourself a rave review if deserved—and even build into your plan some mini rewards—to encourage you as you work towards the big goals. Look over your list outlining the important things in your life. Re-examine your goals to see where the flame lies. Did last week get out of control because of the demands of others; if so, how can you regain control and get back to *your* demands and *your* shoulds?

Analyze this last week with an eye for organizing the coming week. As an organizational tool, try using a chart where you list all possible or known appointments and general meetings. Then list all your goals/priorities for the week (on a "to do" list) and begin to sketch them in for the week—again, giving attention to personal and professional needs. This is an overall plan for a seven-day period and will serve as a guide to your daily self-management charts.

Arrange the details of your week on a daily basis. Schedule set times for meetings and activities requiring specific hours of the day. However, do not assign specific times to all tasks. For example: 10–11 A.M.—make prospecting calls. If an unavoidable interruption occurs from 10:10 to 11:00, the tendency is to continue at 11:00 with your assignment written down for 11:00 to 12:00, "forgetting" that the prospecting calls were not made. Do not let your daily schedule become a means of avoiding unpleasant and difficult "A" priority items. Throughout your day you will refer to your "to do" list, always choosing the top "A" priority to begin working on.

As you plot your week's activities, do not plan on others to satisfy your goals. While you may be sharing common goals, do not plan on and *depend* on others for your goal satisfaction. This insistence on independence is the only way you can become autonomous and responsible for your own life's happiness. Relying on others for goal satisfaction is a dependence on external factors over which you ultimately have little control. Goal satisfaction and accomplishment is controlled from within yourself at the source of your flame of motivation. Plan your week to include others, but evaluate the week just past on the basis of your success and not the contributions or responsiveness of others.

Let's pause for a minute and make sure we both understand something: Yes—this is and will continue to be difficult. Let's not pretend we are talking

about "Ten Easy Steps to Guaranteed Happiness." Those approaches are numerous, tempting, popular—and doomed to failure. This time around we are talking about success, and we are defining success as self-centered—taking charge of our life to do with it what we want. This is not an easy state to achieve. It probably demands some changes—change is always difficult. But then the success hopefully is all the sweeter, and the price for a lack of control over your life is far greater—loss of self esteem.

The achievement of a goal is a wish come to reality.

Touchstones on the Path

Your list of priorities is your map showing the way. Your goals are the compass to keep your course true. The flame of motivation is the fuel to propel you forward. As you travel, use these touchstones to keep you going:

Maintain the Intention to Achieve

Keep your desire high by analyzing what you are doing in terms of where you want to be. Only when you really want to accomplish your goal will the flame within burn bright enough to provide motivation. Maintain goals as yours and not someone else's.

Focus Your Attention on Your Goal

Isolate your goals and visualize them apart from other activities with lesser priority which will be competing for time, attention, and energy. This is why your goals are in writing.

Formulate a Plan of Action

You have the desire to achieve, your attention is clearly focused, now ask yourself: what is my plan for reaching that goal? What must I do to get to the point of accomplishment? Be specific and write it down. Refer to your plan daily and adjust it constantly as you go so that all activities will produce forward motion.

Do It!

Think about your plan and think about carrying it through and then move—begin your journey—now is the time to act—today—not tomorrow. Just as each day precedes and is followed by another, so also each act builds for the future only when a repetition of effort continues. To have followed your plan today is a start, not an end. Repetition is the mortar holding together the building blocks of success.

Take the Action to Completion

Stick with it. Don't lose interest or re-focus on something else until you make the plan work. When your goal is to sell two houses a month, don't stop when you can only sell one a month. It is not important how long it takes before you can consistently sell two a month. It does not matter how often you fall short; the payoff comes when you achieve the goal. Work through a good plan until it performs as you know it can. You conceived the idea. You believed in it. Now achieve it.

Reward Yourself for Accomplishment

A reward is the stroke for the accomplishment of the goal. Be good to yourself, be your own best friend. Reward yourself for a job well done; relax and enjoy it!

Chapter 4

Prospecting

Consider:

For most people the following is true:

Task:	Prospecting
Feeling:	Dislike/fear
Action:	Nothing
Result:	No listings/no sales

For successful agents this is what will work:

Task:	Prospecting
Feeling:	Accept and recognize whatever your negative feeling is
Action:	Rejection-free prospecting = deciding what you can do to contact people that will not result in rejection
Result:	Success—listings/sales

By *not* overlooking *your* very real feelings about prospecting, you determine a way to both meet your goals (successful sales) and take care of your feelings. You are on your way to success—success that deals with two realities—the difficulty of prospecting, and your own feelings about prospecting.

Remember, you can't change reality, but you can change the way you deal with it.

Prospecting is your most visible, active, obvious, and necessary activity as a real estate agent. It can easily be said—if you don't prospect, you won't make it.

Yet, why do so many agents have such a hard time motivating themselves to prospect? One reason—fear of rejection. Prospecting requires talking with people, and anytime you initiate communication, you risk being rejected—especially when you are in sales. And no one wants to be rejected.

What would happen, however, if these same people knew of a way to prospect that was rejection free?

There would probably be many more successful sales agents.

Most agents know how to prospect, but most don't know how to organize their prospecting so they have the least likelihood of meeting rejection. And if you don't have a way to control and minimize rejection, you probably won't prospect.

But as of now, you have no more excuses, because this chapter is organized to help you do just that—control and minimize rejection. You're on your way to rejection-free prospecting.

First, What Exactly Is Prospecting?

Prospecting is the activity of sorting through all the possible people you come in contact with to "earmark" those who are potential clients for buying or selling a home. You may limit this by prospecting a specific part of town or type of home. To help organize your efforts and focus on the right people to contact, keep in mind that the following techniques are used by most successful sales associates:

1. Building a personal referral system

2. Working a "farm"

3. Contacting F.S.B.O.'s (for sale by owner)

4. Contacting expired listings

So What Is Rejection-Free Prospecting?

Rejection-free prospecting is a prospecting technique for anyone who avoids prospecting out of fear of rejection. Assuming that's most of us, this technique is your key to success. It works like this:

1. Rather than *asking* the prospect for anything—you *give* them valuable information, useful hand-outs, your card, a brochure, etc., etc. You do this frequently and regularly.

2. Get your name (and ultimately yourself) in front of them and relate your name to your service. At some time, most people sell and/or buy a home—usually quite a few times in a life span. You want them to think of you.

3. Build up a series of positive experiences with your prospect before risking anything (i.e. asking for something).

As you continue with this chapter, you will learn specific applications of this rejection-free technique for each category of prospecting. These techniques are proven and will work for you, yet require your own imagination and style to carry them through. Your challenge will simply be to make them personal to your needs and your prospect's needs.

1. Building a Personal Referral System

What Is a Personal Referral?

Personal referrals are:

a. Anyone you meet or know who could refer business to you.

b. Unbeatable. They're your best source of buyers and sellers.

The mechanics of establishing a personal referral system are easy. The key to its success is your ability to consistently follow through with your program. All you need is a card file and a big stack of cards.

Setting Up the System

Take the stack of index cards and write down the referral's name, phone number, address, type of relationship or contact. Continue on with as many cards as possible, listing name after name of people who would recognize you if you called them on the phone. Include friends, relatives, past business associates, past clients. Expand your list to include members of social or civic organizations to which you belong. (*see sample*)

Keep this file box on your desk as a daily reminder that here sits your largest source of real estate business.

Prospecting card

Name:	
Address:	
Phone #:	
Dates of contact	Reason for contact
Comments:	

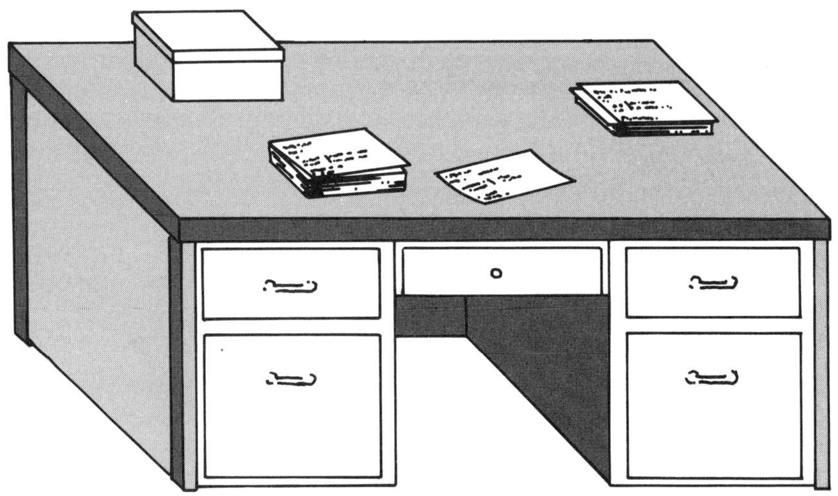

Applying the Rejection-Free System

Be Visible

According to statistical research, people usually only call one real estate agent when listing a home and they list with you, as a person, not a company. So you will need to be visible to these contacts to maximize the possibility that you will be the one they choose. In order to maximize visibility, make sure you do the things which will keep you in their mind. For example: attend meetings regularly, socialize frequently, etc. Always add new contacts to your list whenever you meet someone. Remember, your list is never finished: if you meet someone today, you can add him or her to your growing number of personal contacts. Always update your cards to show when referrals were received. While you may never hear from most of these people, the few who do make referrals (and there are always a few) are worth their weight in gold. As you cultivate these relationships, they will turn into steady sources of referrals.

Call

Call these people three to four times per year. The call should not be lengthy and should have a purpose. Do not ask for anything but state a useful purpose for the call. Some ideas are:

1. A buyers/sellers tax seminar (hosted at your office or in a rented meeting room)

2. A tax update concerning home/property taxes (this could be a brochure that you prepare with the latest information and examples of how it applies to typical homeowners.)

3. A discount program—this works by an arrangement with local businesses who agree to give a discount to anyone who presents one of your coupons. You offer those coupons, redeemable at various local businesses, to your contacts. The businesses send you the coupons, once used, and you follow-up to see if those people would like more coupons. This gives you contact with both referral sources and potential prospects. *See samples.*

Consumer Discount Program

ALARM SYSTEMS

A ALARMS
Call 296-3723
15%

CENTRAL SECURITY ALARM CO. INC.
2817 San Mateo N.E.
15%

AUTOMOTIVE

G & C AUTOMOTIVE
9417 E. Central
10%

BIG-O-TIRES
1141 Juan Tabo N.E.
5%

422 FOREIGN AUTO PARTS, INC.
6115 Richfield N.E.
10%

MURPHY-DORN INC.
Radios, Cruise Controls,
Vinyl Tops & Sunroofs
5620 Osuna N.E.
10%

RICH FORD LEASING, INC.
8601 Lomas Blvd. N.E.
50% off the price of a Maintenance
Agreement on FORD CARS

RICH FORD RENTAL
Car or Truck Rental
815 Osuna N.E.
20%

THE TINT FACTORY
5000 Jefferson N.E.
10%

BOOT & SHOE REPAIR

ACADEMY BOOT & SHOE REPAIR
5901-F Wyoming N.E.
10%

BUILDING MATERIALS

FRANK'S ORNAMENTAL IRON
1619 2nd St. N.W. 843-9367
10%

MOBILE SCREEN & GLASS CO.
8650 Indian School Rd. N.E.
5%

CARPETS

RABY'S CARPET
900 Griegos Rd. N.W
5%

CARPET CLEANING

ALBUQUERQUE CLEANING SPECIALISTS
3600-C Menaul N.E.
20%

CLARK'S SPRINGTIME
5600-H McLeod N.E.
20%

HAWKINS CARPET CLEANING
3600-C Menaul N.E.
10%

PEGASUS CARPET CARE
11405 Nassau N.E.
15%

CLOTHING

BOBETTE'S FASHIONS
3100 Juan Tabo N.E.
10%

CAMILLE'S INC.
1625 San Pedro N.E.
10%

CHARLOTTE'S BOUTIQUE, INC.
5901-X Wyoming N.E.
10%

MARIA'S FASHIONS
6300 San Mateo N.E.
10%

SANDRA BOUTIQUE
5011 Menaul N.E.
10%

SUNBIRD INC.
401 A San Felipe N.W.
Old Town
10%

DENTISTS

DR. ROBERT W. GRODNER DDS
500 Central Ave. S.E.
5%

R.L. DAVISON DDS
7520 Montgomery N.E. E-4
10%

FLORISTS

ANNETTE'S SILK FLOWER ARRANGEMENTS
517 Nathan S.E.
10%

COUNTRY FLOWERS
1111 Corrales Rd. N.W.
10%

EXECUTIVE FLORIST
6233 Montgomery Blvd. N.E.
10%

WIN'S SHOWERS OF FLOWERS
8200 Montgomery N.E.
10%

FOODS

HAKEEM'S IMPORTED FOODS
5850 Osuna N.E.
10%

JAO JAO'S PLACE
5000 Central S.E.
10%

GIFT SHOPS

ANGELINA'S COUNTRY STORE, INC.
3625 Wyoming N.E.
10%

CHEZEM'S GIFT SHOP
2106 Juan Tabo N.E.
10%

K.R.DRUGS INC.
800 I Juan Tabo N.E.
Manzano Center
20%

SCHELU
306 San Felipe N.W.
Old Town
10% on Pottery

THE KHYBER PASS, INC.
2276 Wyoming N.E.
10% (reg. prices only)

TURTLE SHELL GIFTS
8208 Montgomery N.E.
10%

ZARFAS LUGGAGE AND GIFTS
100 Coronado Center
10%

HAIR SALONS & COSMETICS

ACADEMY PLAZA BEAUTY SALON
4410 Wyoming N.E.
10%

AQUARIUS SCULPTURED NAILS
9901 Lomas N.E., Suite G
10%

COSMOS HAIR CONCEPTS
Diana & Antonette
2721 San Mateo N.E.
10%

TERI BRIARLY STUDIO - LION'S MANE HAIR
9405 Menaul N.E.
10%

THE HAIRAFTER
5555 Montgomery N.E. #20
10%

SAL'S HAIR DESIGN
11926 Candelaria N.E.
20%

SHEAR DESIGNS
2521 San Pedro N.E.
Sally Nioya
20%

SPECIAL EFFECTS
5013 Menaul N.E.
10% Hair, Skin & Nails

TOWERS BEAUTY SALON
5400 Montgomery Blvd. N.E.
25%

HOME FURNISHINGS

CLASSIC FANS & FURNISHINGS
Ceiling Fans and Furnishings
5005 Menaul N.E.
25%

FABRIC WORKS
2935-A Louisiana N.E.
15% on Wall & Window
Treatments & Hangings

NAKED FURNITURE
1105 San Mateo N.E.
10%

OAKIQUES
4646 Menaul N.E.
5%

SOFA BLOCK
4636 Menaul N.E.
5%

SYMTEL SATELLITE TELEVISION SYSTEMS
5400 San Mateo Blvd. N.E.
10%

WATERBED PRESCRIPTION
5811 Menaul N.E.
10%

HOME REMODELING

AMIGOS UPHOLSTERY
4730-A Jefferson N.E.
10%

CUSTOM CABINETS
524 El Paraiso N.E.
5%

J.D. GALLEGOS CONSTRUCTION
Concret Work
12337 Claremont N.E.
10%

REMODELING CONTRACTORS INC.
712 Parkside N.E.
10%

HOT TUBS & SPAS

FAMILY POOLS & SPAS
5400 San Mateo Blvd.
10%

HERMANSON & HILL POOLS, SPAS & SUPPLIES
6231 Montgomery N.E.
10%

MOSSMAN-GLADDEN HOT TUBS & SPAS
2700 San Mateo N.E.
5%

JEWELRY

CHANDLER JEWELERS
1120 Montgomery N.E. #29
10%

JEWEL BOX LTD.
6300 San Mateo N.E.
10%

KRUGERS APPRAISALS
3248 San Mateo N.E.
10%

KRUGERS JEWELRY FACTORY OUTLET
3248 San Mateo N.E.
5%

LANDSCAPING

ALBUQUERQUE LAWN & EDGING
5700 Osuna N.E.
7%

LOEPER LANDSCAPING AND NURSERY
5500 San Mateo N.E.
5%

**ROADRUNNER LAWNMOWER & CHAINSAW SALES
& SERVICE**
5600-F McLeod N.E.
6921 Montgomery N.E.
10%

LOCKS & KEYS

ROADRUNNER LOCK/KEY SALES & SERVICE
5600-F McLeod N.E.
6921 Montgomery N.E.
10%

MEMORABILIA

ALBUQUERQUE COLLECTOR'S WORLD
2242 Wyoming Mall N.E.
15% (all items except gold/silver bullion)

OFFICE SUPPLY

BELEW'S OFFICE SUPPLY, INC.
6300 San Mateo N.E.
1724 Lomas N.E.
10% (reg. prices only)

OPTICIANS

COLLINS OPTICAL
11024 Montgomery N.E
Juan Tabo Plaza   298-8008
10%

PEST CONTROL

EXTERMINATOR PEST CONTROL
517 Nathan S.E.
5%

WEST MESA PEST CONTROL
405 Veja Baja Dr. (Rio Rancho)
10%

PHOTOGRAPHY

ONE HOUR PHOTO EXPRESS
304 Coronado Center
10%

PHYSICAL FITNESS CENTERS

NAUTILUS FITNESS CENTERS
All Fitness Centers
10%

PRINTING

AAA EXPRESS PRESS
4503 Menaul N.E.
10%

DESIGN, PRINTING & DISTRIBUTION
4111-A Louisiana N.E.
10%

RECREATIONAL EQUIPMENT

EIGHT BALL BILLIARD SUPPLY
5622 Menaul N.E.
6% (reg. prices only)

RENTALS

RENTAL DATA
3004 Central Ave. N.E. #D
20%

RESTAURANTS

EL PATRON
2266 Wyoming N.E.
10%

TAXIDERMY

MUSEUM TAXIDERMY
8009 Central N.E.
5%

HOOTEN/STAHL, INC. REALTORS
PARTICIPATION DISCOUNT AGREEMENT

Agreement Date__________

____
Name of Organization

We understand that in return for the promotion of our
business by the associates of Hooten/Stahl, Inc. Realtors,
we agree to the following:

1. All of our staff will be aware of this program.

2. The discount given will be an ACTUAL discount
    available on all merchandise and services. The
    discount will be given only with the presentation
    of the Hooten/Stahl Consumer Discount Certificate.

3. All customers presenting the Certificate will
    receive our usual excellent service.

4. All referrals from our organization will be re-
    ferred to Hooten/Stahl, Inc. Realtors.

5. We and the associates of Hooten/Stahl, Inc.
    Realtors understand that the intent of this
    agreement is to create a reciprocal referral
    system between the two parties.

6. Our agreement with you will continue automatically
    unless a 30 day written notification is given by
    either party.

Business Address____

Discount_______%

Signature Owner/Manager_________________________________

Hooten/Stahl Sales Associate____________________________

▶◀Z HOOTEN/STAHL, INC.

41

4. Wishing them a Merry Christmas, Happy Easter, etc.

5. Whatever ideas you can create that will get your name in front of people. (New listings, investment opportunities, etc.)

After making your offer, thank them for their time, indicate you will be in contact again. Good-bye. Short. To the point. A minimum of interruption for the contact. And, most important, non-threatening for you because you are not "selling" anything, you are just keeping in touch because you can provide a service to someone who may need it. Simple.

Visit

Schedule your time so you will stop by their house two times per year (especially those people who have already referred someone to you). Don't plan a lengthy visit; simply say—you were in the neighborhood and wanted to say hello. Avoid unrealistic expectations—for example, that people will invite you in and give you a referral on the spot. Understand that this visit is one part of keeping your name current with your contacts. Again, you are not "selling" anything, only maintaining visibility.

Mailings

Your last responsibility in setting up a personal referral program is mailings—frequent, consistent, long-term mailings. The best program is one which sends one piece of literature (a letter, tax information form, postcard) every other week to every person in your referral box. One mailing is a waste—don't bother. Statistics show 55 percent of the people who receive "junk mail" read it; 12 percent even enjoy reading it. They may not read every word, probably just enough to get the general idea. But, when they receive a company mailing with your name on it every other week, their awareness of your existence as a real estate agent will be heightened.

Contact Summary

- 26 mailings a year
- 2 personal visits a year
- 4 phone calls per year
- constant visibility in the community.

This is how you maximize your chances of "being there" when your contact becomes aware of someone who is moving.

Don't stop yet. Your efficient follow up at this point will mean repeat referrals from this same person.

Efficient follow up means:

- First, showing your appreciation with a gift or a sincere statement of thanks.
- Then, keeping the person informed. A short call as you progress from initial appointment through final closing will reassure your contact and afford another opportunity to express your appreciation.
- Sending information regularly and perhaps stopping by his home throughout this period.
- When the transaction is concluded, calling your contact and letting her/him know.

Each of these contacts is only one part of your total effort. And the effectiveness of this phase is greatly magnified because it is part of a continuing program.

As you schedule your time, remember your priorities: your number one source of business is from personal referrals. Make time to properly take care of your number one priority. Keep your referral box on top of your desk and regularly make calls whenever you have a few minutes. That is all it takes to keep in touch. But it is kind of like painting the Golden Gate bridge—you are never done. It is an on-going, continuous process but one which will do the most for helping you attain success in the real estate business.

2. Working a Farm

What Is Farming?

Farming is selecting a specific area of homes and concentrating your efforts in that area.

Why Do You Want to Farm?

a. *To build a clientele*

Just like a doctor or lawyer, farming allows you to take a more professional approach to your business by building a following of people with whom you work. It gives you control—you choose with whom you want to work.

b. *To increase your income*

Yes—you will get listings through professional, regular farming contacts. No—they will not come overnight. It's not realistic to even expect farming to pay off after one month.

Warning: Be careful not to say: if I don't get a listing "soon" I'm going to quit farming. It will probably take four to six months before you see the first flower. In farming, you are planting seeds for the future; the odds are slim for immediate gain. You will not be disappointed if you accept this reality.

c. *To stabilize income*

Once you have a reliable core clientele you will be in good shape financially with a steady flow of listings providing a basis of income.

d. *To become an expert*

You cannot become an expert on an entire city; it is simply too large. But you can become an expert on your farm area. Most people know little about real estate in their neighborhood. Your objective is to become the neighborhood expert to fill this information gap.

How Do You Farm Successfully?

You *earn the right* to sell someone's house and you do that best by providing information and by being available. (For specifics, see the Ten Steps of Farming, pages 48–51.)

The Problem with Farming

Most sales associates know how important it is to farm; it is the *second best source of business*—but dread it—to the point that they do not do it regularly enough to really make it pay off.

Most of us have tried it. You gear yourself up to spend a day walking your farm area. You look sharp, feel prepared to present yourself and your company as *the* real estate professional in your area. You chart your course and hopefully approach that first door. You knock, smile pleasantly and are greeted with indifference. You introduce yourself and ask for their business or a personal referral. No. Nothing. Go away. On to the next house. Same approach, same smiling introduction and questions, same bored or angry response. But you can handle it and so continue to a few more homes. By the fourth or fifth indifferent or annoyed response, you begin to question your credentials. Do I look okay? Am I too pushy? Too laid back? I just want to help these people, but why am I not making them understand?

You may try a couple more, but you know you are ready to call it a day when you start choosing homes because it looks like no one is in. You decide this is not working, you will never get any business this way. You go back to the office to see what is going on there. Later in the day it begins to sink in: farming is so important but you are not any good at it. People do not respond well to you. They rejected you time after time. You begin to feel guilty about your inadequacies.

Yet, hopefully, you will try again. You really like people and do not mind knocking on doors and chatting with strangers. It is the *rejection* you cannot take.

A Rejection-Free Farming Scenario

So—try changing tactics. Try this rejection-free farming strategy: Knock on a stranger's door. Introduce yourself and give the homeowner some printed information about tax savings, property values in the area or anything that may be appropriate. Thank him for his time, wish him a nice day. Good-bye. Who knows if they have rejected you or not—you were not there long enough to find out. But the homeowner now has something with your name on it for at least a few minutes before throwing it out.

That is the basis of rejection-free farming: you cannot be rejected because you are not asking for anything. You are simply supplying information on a regular basis. *Repetition* is the ingredient that makes the system work.

Note: Other approaches will also work given enough repetition. But one problem is: approaches relying on positive responses to direct questions ("Do you know anyone who is moving that I might contact?") are just too hard on the old self-esteem to make repeating the process a real possibility. Most of us simply cannot handle repeated rejections. Yet we can meet and greet . . . and then move on. So you can farm.

TAX ANALYSIS WORKSHEET

1. BASIS OF OLD RESIDENCE AMOUNT

A. Purchase Price $ _____
B. Less Personal Property – _____
C. Net Purchase Price (A-B) _____
D. Acquisition Costs

_____ $ _____

Total Acquisition Costs: + _____
E. Total Investment Price (C+D) _____
F. Less Cumulative Deferred Gain– _____
G. Total Basis of
Old Residence (E-F) $ _____

2. CAPITAL IMPROVEMENTS

Date: Improvement
_____ $ _____

A. Total Capital Improvements: $ _____

3. ENERGY EXPENDITURES AMOUNT

(See Separate Worksheet on Reverse)
A. Total Energy Expenditures
To Be Added To Basis $ _____

4. ADJUSTED BASIS

A. Total Basis of Old Residence (Item 1G) $ _____
B. Total Capital Improvements (Item 2A) + _____
C. Energy Expenditures (Item 3A) + _____
D. Adjusted Basis $ _____

5. SELLING EXPENSES

_____ $ _____

A. Total Selling Expenses: $ _____

6. GAIN FROM SALE

A. Sale Price $ _____
B. Less Personal Property – _____
C. Net Sales Price (A-B) _____
D. Less Selling Expenses (Item 5A) – _____
E. Amount Realized (C-D)
F. Less Adjusted Basis (Item 4D) – _____
G. Realized Gain (E-F) $ _____

7. ADJUSTED SALES PRICE AMOUNT

A. Amount Realized (Item 6E) $ _____
B. Fix-Up Expenses
Date: Description:

_____ $ _____

Less Total Fix-Up Expenses - _____
C. Adjusted Sales Price (A-B) $ _____

8. GAIN RECOGNIZED

A. Adjusted Sales Price (Item 7C) $ _____
B. Less **Net** Purchase Price Plus
Acquisition Costs of New Property – _____
C. Gain Recognized (A-B) Taxable $ _____

*If 8B is greater than 8A enter 0
**Taxable Gain is Lesser of Item 8C or Item 6G

9. DEFERRED GAIN

A. Realized Gain (Item 6G) $ _____
B. Less Gain Recognized (Item 8c) – _____
C. Deferred Gain (A-B) $ _____

10. BASIS IN NEW RESIDENCE

A. **Net** Purchase Price + Acquisition
Costs of New Property (Item 8B) $ _____
B. Less Deferred Gain (Item 9C) – _____
C. Total Basis in New Residence (A-B) $ _____

THE LARGEST TAX YOU'LL EVER FACE!

The largest tax most homeowners will ever face is one you may not even be aware of. We're talking about the tax on all the profits ever realized from all the home sales over your lifetime.

The IRS code states that any profit, from whatever source, shall be taxed. That includes any gains realized from residential sales.

When you sell a home, it's like selling stocks and bonds. If you sell at a profit, you expect to pay a Capital Gains tax; however, if you purchase another home soon after selling, at a higher price, the tax on any profit is postponed, or deferred.

After selling a home, most homeowners buy "up" in price, postponing tax after tax. Because these taxes are often deferred for years, the owner often forgets about them. Needless to say, the IRS does not forget!

Home prices tripled over the past 10 years, creating enormous profits for homeowners. Most experts predict a continuing of this price spiral. Today, after a lifetime of ownership, many sellers face a tax on accumulated profits of $150,000, $200,000 or more.

At today's rates, the tax could easily run 15-20% or higher. That is why we say it will probably be the largest tax you'll ever face.

To cut these taxes drastically, report the lowest profit possible on each sale. Most homeowners don't realize that many expenses incurred allow them to report a lower profit to the IRS.

You must start a sound record-keeping system now, and continue it throughout your lifetime. The Creative Real Estate Services Tax Program offers such a system.

Our "Homeowner Tax Guide" makes it clear. It illustrates each area where records are vital. Included in each guide is the Homeowner Tax Analysis form which can be used to report each sale in the most advantageous manner.

We can't guarantee you a dollar amount of saving. But we can assure you that you will pay the least amount of tax possible, and in most cases the savings can run into thousands of dollars.

Don't wait another day. Start your tax-saving system today to minimize that largest of all tax obligations.

Look for our Homeowner Tax Newsletter every other month.

James K. DuVal © 1983

Ten Rejection-Free Steps of Farming

Farming can be summarized into the following steps:

Step #1: Select Your Farm Carefully

Choose an area with similar properties so you will be able to compare prices of homes and point out the relative value of homes in the area. A high 'turn-over' rate is also desirable.

Do not include "too many" homes in your farm area. Do not play the numbers game: if 300 homes will get me "X" number of listings, 450 homes will net even more. Not true. Remember, a successful farming program relies on mailings *and* personal contact. Can you really and realistically call on 450 homes four to six times per year? Mailings *alone* will not do it. Quality of effort is crucial; it is better to have 150 homeowners with whom you keep in contact rather than 450, half of whom you never see.

People move an average of once every five years. That means in a farm area of 300 homes there will be sixty possible listings per year! Of course, you will not get them all. Aim for your share of these sixty listings based on doing a really good job with fewer homes rather than a poor job with more homes.

Step #2: Develop a Farm Record System

Establish a system for keeping records on properties and homeowners. This should serve as a reference tool for planning mailings and "earmarking" appropriate dates for personal calls. This reference is made up of *property farming cards* and *owner farming cards.* The property farming card includes addresses, names, phone numbers, and sales information; the owner farming card lists for each owner birthdays, children, pets, interests, etc. These logs of homes and personalities may be useful to some and unnecessary for others. Tailor your particular needs to your own style of working. You will probably find you need some method of "keeping track," but it may be more or less detailed than someone else's method.

Step #3: Set Up a Farm Map

You said you were going to farm to become an expert in your area: so— be an expert. Know what is going on. A map of your farm area placed in an obvious part of your work setting will help you a great deal. Use colored pins to mark your listings and sales and competitors' listings and sales. Stay aware of what is happening in your farm area. In time, you will see more of your pins and less of theirs.

Step #4: Send Letters of Introduction

This is a way to make that first contact. It should reflect you and the image you want to project and it should be short and to the point. The most advisable format is probably the postcard, since the homeowner will surely toss it after a quick glance. The message should state that you are a specialist in this neighborhood and close by committing you to action. Write that you will be stopping by in a few weeks to say hello, and you will mentally be committed to following through—it will be less likely to be put off to some indefinite future. Do not include personal information on yourself; remember, the homeowner really does not care. Your objective is to focus the potential prospect's attention on your name and purpose.

Step #5: Make Telephone Follow-Up Calls

All the steps until now have been totally rejection-free. However, it takes a little more planning effort to keep it that way when making telephone calls. You need to focus on your purpose in calling. You are not soliciting anything; you do not want anything. Simply introduce yourself, remind them of your note (they should have received), of your upcoming short visit, and of the fact that you are a real estate specialist in their area. Be *brief,* friendly, and honest. This is not a sales call. You will not get a listing from this one phone call and your program is not a failure because you did not get a listing. This call is *one step* in a cumulative campaign designed to do one thing—associate your name with real estate. Period. (When the person needs to sell his house, you may— or may not—get the listing. But when this connection is repeatedly made to 300 homeowners, you *will* get your share of the sixty listings per year that develop in your farm area.)

Step #6: Send Thank You Notes

A short follow-up card received a few days after your phone call is a nice, personal touch. Thank the person for being so pleasant on the phone. This encourages him to continue to be pleasant.

Note: At this point, be careful to organize your time carefully. This note does not have to be hand-written. If you plan to write each one yourself it probably won't get done. That's reality. Hire someone to process your mailings so you do not get all hung up in technical details. This note is short and sweet, but will produce results by helping to reduce resistance to your upcoming personal visit. You have shown you are not hard-sell, tricky, or long-winded. You have set the stage for the purpose of your visit. The homeowner will probably feel less inclined to be defensive and negative.

Step #7: Make Personal Contact

Inevitably there comes the day you must begin your "cold canvas" of the area. But it is not quite as cold because you have written these people and you have already talked to them on the phone. You have set yourself up as a professional with a specific purpose. Begin your visit by introducing yourself and your company, then give them your card. You may want to develop other "hand-out" items for subsequent visits; the important thing is to give them something with your name on it. (See Step #10.) Be complimentary about their home and neighborhood (if you can do so with honesty and sincerity). Be pleasant and show interest in what they may have to say. Mention your specialization in their area, but do not solicit a listing. Simply give information, and don't stay too long.

Note: Practice your dialogue before you approach your first few homes to make sure your delivery is smooth.

Remember: the aim of farming is *not* to develop listings; the purpose is to get appointments. Since 78 percent of all potential listers only call one broker for a presentation, you are increasing your chances of being the one called by making the contact and the connection.

If you still think you will have trouble with making this personal contact, shorten the format. Do not even try to engage them in conversation of any sort. Just knock on the door, introduce yourself, leave your business card and say good-bye. This will still be better than no contact at all and will still be an effective link in your consistent farming program. It will put a face—a real person—behind the voice on the phone and the name on the card. It will not be successful *all by itself*—but it does not have to be.

Step #8: Send Thank You Notes

"Thanks for being so pleasant when I called on you the other day." Another step in making the connection between *you* and your real estate service.

Step #9: Work Your Farm

Here is the step with the most room for your own personal style and creativity. You will want a list of items to pass out regularly to maintain contact. The type or value of the item is <u>not</u> important; the fact that it comes every two months makes it an effective selling tool. Some ideas: door hangers passed out by neighborhood kids; new listing cards on area homes; new neighbor introductions; service directory of local people interested in baby sitting, yard work, etc.; free drawings for turkeys or T-shirts; seasonal pumpkins, balloons, candy canes, spring seeds, tax analysis forms. Whatever ideas you develop, it will not pay to even consider a mailing or distribution just one time. You must plan a consistent, regular program.

Remember: You must earn the right to sell someone's home and you do that best by providing information and by being available.

Step #10: Follow These Rules

First, be consistent and repetitive. Remember, the key to successful farming
is repetition.

Second, deal with the people who are home. If you are unable to make contact
with a homeowner, why keep them in your farm? Personal contact is
part of a successful farming program.

Third, eliminate the negative. If someone is rude and unreceptive to your call,
eliminate them from your farm. Also eliminate relatives of other agents.
Why waste your efforts and ego on hostile people or on those who will
refer their business to their brother in the business? Work efficiently and
positively to eliminate these negative and unproductive calls.

Fourth, follow up with a thank you note after every contact with a homeowner.
This is how you "stay in touch."

Fifth, become a friend of the area by attending neighborhood functions such
as homeowners meetings, local fund raisings, block parties. Your in-
volvement and visibility at a meeting brings you in contact with twenty
or so people in your farm area, many of whom would love to have an
agent at the meeting to keep them aware of market trends in their neighborhood.

Sixth,—and probably most important—plan to personally see everyone in your
farm area about every sixty days. While severe weather or a heavy business season may extend the time between personal contacts to ninety
days or so, if you have planned your program carefully you will be able
to fill in with a substitute contact (door hangers, special mailings, etc.)
until you can get back to your personal contact schedule.

Remember that timing is crucial to your successful farming program.
If you have maintained contact with your homeowners, if you have established
your name with the business of real estate, if you repeatedly, frequently and
consistently present your name and your business, then when the time comes
for the homeowner to plan for a move, you will have greatly increased your
chances for being called. You will have demonstrated your interest and professionalism and will have earned the right to be considered as their listing agent.

If you have conducted your program successfully, you will have established this awareness among all 300 people in your farm area.

Payoff for Farming

Three hundred families who move once every five years equals sixty
houses per year going up for sale. Will you get all sixty listings? No. Would
you be happy with ten, fifteen, twenty listings? Of course! Is this a realistic

expectation of the success of your farming program? Yes! That's fifteen listings in addition to the buyers you already work with (and fifteen listings in addition to your personal referral business).

Farming is not "easy." It takes time, organization and consistent follow through. It takes discipline to set up your program and do it year after year. Remember, families in your farm move once every five years. You may be contacting some households for as long as five years, although it is realistic to see returns within six to twelve months.

And the nicest part of the program is that it is "rejection-free" and—when you work—it works.

3. Contacting FSBO's

A Few FSBO Statistics:

43% . . . list with a friend. You never had a chance for this listing.—

19% . . . will sell their home by themselves. Again, you never had a chance.

17% . . . did not sell their home and finally just took it off the market.

21% . . . listed with a Realtor who knocked on their door.

The Problem with FSBO's

When you go to a For Sale By Owner home and knock on the door, who do you expect to see? Not just with your eye, but with your mind's eye—with that part that includes your feelings and preconceptions?

Do you expect to see a great hairy monster? Someone who will slam the door in your face after throwing a bucket of water at you? Someone terribly annoyed by "another" real estate agent telling him he cannot possibly sell his house without the help of a "professional"? Does this vision so intimidate you that you ignore your *number three source of business?* Have you convinced yourself it would be unprofitable—in terms of both time and shattered ego—to waken the sleeping ogre of FSBO?

Wait a minute. Take a close look at the next person to enter the room you're in. Imagine him or her as a FSBO—just a person trying to sell his house without going through a real estate office. Not a mean person, but a person who simply wants to save the real estate commission, and is fairly confident he can handle the transaction.

Avoiding Rejection with FSBO's

The trick is—don't ask if you can sell his house. And do not tell him what your company can do for him; he thinks he does not *need* your company, so if you tell him he does, he will only further reject you—for not listening to what he just said. Your *only goal* in contacting the FSBO is to develop some rapport—an affinity. Let him know who you are and that you are a friendly, helpful person.

Rejection-Free Steps for Working with FSBO's

Here is your program:

Step 1. Identify a For Sale By Owner home.

Step 2. Knock on the door. Say hello and introduce yourself. Acknowledge to yourself that many real estate agents have probably already called and asked for the listing. So, be different—do not solicit.

Step 3. Give one piece of material with information helpful to the seller (perhaps a flyer on Better Ways to Show His Home). Say thank you and leave. (*See samples*)

Step 4. Repeat Step 3 once a week for as long as the home is on the market.

Do not worry that your approach is not fancy or that your pamphlet is not slick and stylized. *Do not* ask for anything; if you do not ask you cannot be rejected. *Do not* create negative feelings by insisting the house cannot be sold without your help.

The key to getting the listing is making contact and establishing rapport. The only "close" to use is to ask them if they have any questions. If they do then try to make an appointment to help them. The key to establishing rapport is to provide information that will really help them sell their house by themselves *without* your help. This shows that you heard them and acknowledge their intentions. Remember, statistics show you do not stand a chance with 79 percent of these people in the first place. You are working on the 21 percent who will eventually list with a real estate agent. It is important that you understand these statistics so that you don't have unreasonable expectations. If you don't deal with reality you will have a tendency to question the system or yourself and stop doing it.

IMPORTANT
GUIDELINES TO FOLLOW
WHEN PURCHASING A HOME

YOU CAN HELP

With your understanding of the purchasing process, your transaction can go a lot smoother. This guideline has proven invaluable to purchasers and is worth your special attention.

QUALIFYING

For your benefit, it is essential that I ask questions to understand your needs, wants, and ability to purchase.

SHOWING PROCESS

Please feel free to inspect all facets of a home during its showing. It may be a good idea to note any comments you have about each home in order for me to provide you with the best possible service.

SUGGESTED NUMBER OF HOMES TO VIEW DAILY

I will assist you in selecting homes for viewing in accordance with your family's needs. To avoid confusion, I will show you only 5 to 8 homes at one time.

COMMUNICATIONS WITH SALES ASSOCIATE

Feedback is essential in providing maximum service. Specific comments about each home will help me determine exactly what you are seeking.

MAKING AN OFFER

As a result of our communication and my professionalism, many of my buyers have been able to find a suitable home in a short period of time. Making an offer will prevent you from losing the home that will give you the most for your money.

PRESENTING THE OFFER

After an offer is written, I will contact the listing salesperson and set up an appointment with the homeowners. I will present the offer to the listing salesperson and sellers as soon as possible. The sellers then have the following alternatives:
1. Accept the offer as presented.
2. Reject the offer.
3. Counter (a change in price, date, personal property, etc.).

If a counter is made, you have the same three alternatives — accept, reject, or counter.

CONTRACT ACCEPTANCE

Once the contract is accepted, I will notify you immediately. At this time you may wish to retain the services of an attorney to represent you, because "it is mutually understood and agreed that, by law, Broker (salesperson) is only permitted to prepare a contract of sale."

MORTGAGE APPLICATION

I will assist you in making contact with a lending institution. It is extremely important that you apply for a mortgage immediately following acceptance of the contract. Some lending institutions may require fees (to be paid at the time of application) for a credit check and appraisal of the property. The lending institution will require information concerning current income and obligations (bank account and charge account numbers). The lending agency will now verify this information and have the property appraised.

PROCESSING OF LOAN

Make sure any information required by the lending institution is supplied to them immediately. This will prevent any delays in obtaining a mortgage commitment. Please allow approximately   days for processing a conventional loan. In the case of FHA, VA, or loans requiring private mortgage insurance, more time may have to be allowed. I will contact you immediately upon notification of mortgage approval.

SIGNING OF MORTGAGE DOCUMENTS AND "BRINGING DOWN TITLE"

When the mortgage is approved, the lending institution will require you to sign mortgage documents. This usually occurs prior to closing. The lending institution will then contact the title insurance company who will do research to establish present condition of title.

TIME AND PLACE OF CLOSING

Although a date for closing is specified in the contract, the lending institution and the attorneys are responsible for determining the actual time and place of closing.

PRIOR TO CLOSING

1. You will have the opportunity to make a final inspection of the property.

2. To eliminate mechanical problems, a 1-year Buyers Protection Plan is available to protect the vital systems of your new home.

3. A paid-up insurance policy and receipt must be brought to closing.

4. A couple of days before closing, the lending institution or attorney will notify you of the closing cost figures. A certified check, cashier's check, or cash must be presented at closing (personal checks not acceptable).

James K. DuVal © 1983

For Sale by Owner
≡*MOVING MEMO*

Change Of Address Checklist

Here is a handy list of all the people you might need to tell about moving. Also, remember to tell close friends and relatives your new address. For those you write to only on Christmas, make a note to send your Christmas cards out very early next year so they know of your new address before they send you their Christmas cards.

Utilities:
- ☐ Electric
- ☐ Gas
- ☐ Water
- ☐ Telephone
- ☐ Fuel

Publications:
- ☐ Newspapers
- ☐ Magazines
- ☐ Professional
- ☐ Fraternal

Government & Public Offices:
- ☐ Veterans Administration
- ☐ Library
- ☐ City Hall-Garbage & Refuse
- ☐ State Motor Vehicle Bureau
- ☐ Social Security Administration
- ☐ State/Federal Income Tax Bureau
- ☐ Post Office
- ☐ Draft Board

Insurance Agencies:
- ☐ Life
- ☐ Fire
- ☐ Auto
- ☐ Home
- ☐ Health
- ☐ Accident
- ☐ Hospital

Professional Services:
- ☐ Doctor
- ☐ Dentist
- ☐ Certified Public Accountant
- ☐ Lawyer
- ☐ Broker

Established Business Accounts:
- ☐ Dry Cleaner
- ☐ Bakery
- ☐ Drug Store
- ☐ Diaper Service
- ☐ Department Stores
- ☐ Water Softener Service
- ☐ Dairy
- ☐ Service Stations
- ☐ Laundry
- ☐ Banks
- ☐ Finance Companies
- ☐ Automobile Agency
- ☐ Real Estate Agency

Miscellaneous:
- ☐ Relatives, Friends
- ☐ Business Associates
- ☐ Book & Record Clubs
- ☐ Organizations & Clubs
- ☐ School
- ☐ Your landlord, if you are a tenant
- ☐ Your tenants, if you are a landlord
- ☐ Church

"We List and Sell More Homes Than Anyone in New Mexico."

Moving With Children

Young children, especially those who have never moved before may be apprehensive about moving, so preparing them for it is most important. Talk to each child. Explain the reason for the move and how he can help make it a success. Try to explain the move on your children's level of understanding and encourage them to express their feelings openly. They may be upset at first, but once they understand that the move is inevitable and that you are counting on them to help, most disagreement will disappear. Explain to them that they will have to leave playmates, school and their room behind. But help them anticipate the new friends and fun that waits for them at your new home.

There are travel and vacation books written about almost everywhere. Find books about your new area and read them to your children. Colorful pictures and descriptions of your new home will make your new location less of a mystery. Write the Chamber of Commerce in your new city. They can provide you with much of this type of information at no charge. Build your children's anticipation.

Involve your children in planning the move. Make sure that they're an integral part of it. Describe how the moving van will carefully pack everything away so that they arrive at your new home safely. Make the move a family project. It's more positive for everyone, including you, that way.

YOUR FIRST VISIT TO YOUR NEW LOCATION

You will probably make at least one househunting trip to your new community. You're going to a strange town where you don't know anyone or your way around. You could easily become confused unless you have prepared for this trip carefully.

Read books and travel literature about your new community. Look at local maps. Read about landmarks. Use information provided you by the local Chamber and your Realtors to plan your trip. Take along a camera too. Take pictures to take back to show your children. The tree that's just waiting for a tree house. The local baseball field or maybe even a shot of the neighbor children that will soon be your kids' playmates. Explain everything to your children carefully. You'll see their enthusiasm build and grow with every new possibility you present them.

For Sale by Owner
MOVING MEMO

Arrival Kit

Here are some suggestions for what you may need upon arriving at your new home. It should be marked "LOAD LAST, UNLOAD FIRST."

Cleaning:
Soap powder
(cleaning agents or aids)
Kitchen cleanser
Dish towels
Paper towels
Dish cloth
Steel wool pads
Sponge
Window cleaner

Snacks:
Easy-open cans of pudding
Sandwich spreads
Jars of cheese
Package of crackers
Instant creamer, sugar, salt
Dry soup mix
Boxes of dry cereals, raisins
Instant coffee, tea, chocolate

Kitchen:
Paper plates, cups, napkins
Plastic knives, forks, spoons
Plastic pitcher for mixing drinks
Small saucepan
Serving spoons

Miscellaneous:
Light bulb or two
Flashlight
Hammer, screwdriver, pliers
Aluminum foil
Shelf paper
Trash bags

Bathroom:
Facial tissue
Toilet tissue
Bath towel
Face cloth
Bath soap
First-aid kit

Children:
Coloring books and crayons
A favorite toy or two
Reading materials
Puzzles

Notes:

Tips On Packing

The biggest extra cost when you move comes from having the moving company do the packing. They charge for both the containers (from $1.00 to $7.00 depending on the size) and for the labor (up to $10.00 an hour). The biggest savings you can make is by doing the packing yourself.

You can probably do as good a job of packing your own household goods as the moving company — but only if you use common sense and follow a few guidelines.

- Use clean, strong containers that are in good condition and that can be secured tightly with twine or strapping tape. (Even if you do the packing yourself, these can usually be purchased from your moving company.)
- Label each box as to contents, which room in the new house it should go in, whether it is fragile, and whether it should be loaded last so as to be unloaded first.
- Don't load more than 50 pounds into any one box, and make sure the weight is evenly distributed throughout the box.
- Cushion contents with newspaper or excelsior to prevent breakage. Use newsprint (newspaper without any printing on it) or tissue paper for items that might be soiled by newspaper.
- Pack books tightly on end in small boxes. Alternate bindings and wrap valuable books separately. If you have a lot of books, consider shipping them parcel post to save money.
- Purchase special boxes from the moving company for dishes, wardrobe, and other special items.
- Have your rugs and draperies cleaned before moving and leave them in their wrappings for easier handling.
- Remove all breakables and liquids from drawers and pack them separately.
- Pack linen, clothing and the like in drawers, but don't overload them or the joints may crack.
- Seal medicines and other containers to prevent leaking and pack in a leakproof bag or container.
- Carry all valuables with you. Don't pack jewelry, documents, coin or stamp collections or anything that will be difficult to replace. Banks can arrange to have contents of safe deposit box moved for you.

For Sale by Owner
MOVING MEMO

Tips On Moving House Plants

If you can't bear the thought of leaving your house plants behind, there are ways you can take them with you without hurting them.

1. Call your local U.S. Department of Agriculture to check on regulations for moving from the state you are now in to the one you are going to. Many states have restrictions on what kinds of plants can be brought into the state. This is to prevent importing of bugs or pests that can destroy valuable cash crops in that state.

2. A few weeks before your move, take plants in clay pots and repot them in unbreakable plastic containers. Plastic containers should be the same size as the clay ones.

3. A couple of weeks before your move, prune plants so they can be easily packed. Consult a florist or a plant book to learn the best way to prune them. This will make the plant easier to move and they will need less water and less sunlight to survive.

4. A week before your move, put your plants in a black plastic bag with a bug/pest strip, conventional flea collar or spray a little bit of bug spray in the bag before you put the plant in. Close the bag and place in a cool area overnight or for about 8 hours. This will help kill any parasites or pests on the plant or in the soil.

5. The day before your move, secure the plants in cardboard containers. Make sure they are held snugly in place by dampened newspaper or packing paper. More paper should be used to cushion the leaves and a final layer of wet paper should be put on top to keep them moist. Water the plants normally in summer, a little less in winter.

6. On the day of your move, set the boxes aside and mark "DO NOT LOAD" so they won't be taken on the moving van by mistake.

7. On the day you leave, close boxes, punch air holes in the top and put in your car where they will be protected.

8. When you are on the road, be careful where you park your car. Park in a shaded area in the summer and a sunny spot in the winter.

9. Unpack the plants as soon as you can after arriving at your new home. Take plants out through the bottom of the box in order to avoid breaking the stems. Do not expose the plants to too much sunlight at first, let them get accustomed to more light gradually.

10. If you don't have space to carry all of your plants, then take cuttings. Put cuttings in a plastic bag with wet paper towels around them.

If you are a plant lover, taking your plants with you will be important. They'll add a touch of coziness to your strange new surroundings and make you feel more at home.

For Sale by Owner
MOVING MEMO

Getting Your House In Shape To Sell

Assuming that all of the major systems such as heating, air conditioning, hot water, appliances, etc. are in working order, you're ready to work on the "impression" aspects of your home. Good maintenance and upkeep really pay off. Don't hesitate to make small cosmetic repairs. Remember, everything shows to someone who is about to make such a large financial investment. Take nothing for granted.

When a potential buyer pulls up to your house, his first impressions will stay with him throughout his househunting. The first impression must be good and strong. The exterior paint should be perfect. Repaint, if necessary. Fresh paint always makes a house look new. Make sure the grass is cut, hedges, bushes, walkways and shrubs are trimmed and cleaned. Clean up any paper or other trash that might have blown into the yard. Also, if it's winter, make sure that the drive and walk are shoveled and kept free of ice and snow. If the buyer has a bad impression of the outside of the house, you have little chance of impressing him with the inside.

Inside your house should be the real selling point. Rooms should be neat, clean and spacious looking. You can make rooms look larger by removing excess furniture and clutter. Cabinets and closets should also be clean. Pack nonessential items. By doing so you accomplish two things: one is to make your cabinet space look much larger, and two, you get some of the drudgery of packing out of the way early.

See that any cracks in the plaster or paint are repaired. Any woodwork such as trim, bookcases, stair railings, etc. should be cleaned and refinished if necessary. Carpets should be shampooed. Bathrooms should be cleaned and polished, chrome and tile especially. The kitchen should be clean and homey looking. Make sure that floors and windows are shining. Drapes should be cleaned. If you have a basement, see that it is dry. Leaky basements are a sure hitch in any sale. If you have gas lights or a gas grill, make sure that they're in working order. Make the interior of your home sparkle. It must look well taken care of and homey. Neatness is the byword here, too.

Don't hedge or take short cuts when preparing your house. If the prospective buyer even suspects that you're trying to cover up a problem, you can count him out as a buyer. Be honest with people who ask probing questions. If you have nothing to hide, your honesty could be the best selling tool you have.

Nothing is more offensive to prospective home buyers than odors and messes associated with pets. If you have a cat, it is a good practice to clean your cat's litter box once a day. Dog owners should make sure their yards are clean too.

For Sale by Owner
MOVING MEMO
Tips On Moving Pets

Live animals cannot be boxed and shipped on a moving van, even for the shortest move. They need special care and handling to get to their new home. Here are a few tips on getting your menagerie from here to there.

FISH

In general, it is impractical to move an aquarium with fish in it. A gallon of water weighs 8 pounds. Plan on giving the fish away with a promise to restock the aquarium when you arrive at your new home.

CATS AND DOGS

Cats and dogs can be moved one of two ways — shipped by air or taken along in the family car.

If you are flying to your new destination, your cat or dog can ride in the baggage compartment. To fly on an airplane, your pet will need a health certificate from your vet. Call the airline in advance to find out about special boxes they may have to hold a pet. If you are going to make a container for it, make sure it complies with the airline's regulations. To make sure the pet is comfortable, it is a good idea to get some tranquilizers from your vet to give it right before going to the airport. It's also a good idea to put a piece of clothing with your scent on it in the animal's box so it will feel more at home.

If you aren't flying with your pet, but are having it shipped by air, make sure someone is on the other end to pick it up at the airport and take care of it until you arrive. The easiest way to ship it is to let a kennel do it for you. Many kennels can take the pet several days before you move (thus keeping it out of your way), box it, take it to the airport and arrange to have a kennel on the other end pick it up and take care of it until you arrive.

Think twice about taking your dog or cat with you on a long cross-country trip. Not only can animals get car-sick like humans, but being cooped up in a car all day can make them nervous and can cause them to act strangely. They must be fed and watered (make sure you take along their water dish), they have to make rest stops and they have to be on a leash to keep them from running off any time the car door is opened.

Some motels and hotels won't allow pets. Others have specially designed facilities for handling travelers' pets. Call in advance and check out the available literature on hotels along your route. National chains usually publish information like this, so check with them too.

SMALLER ANIMALS

Collections of hamsters, birds, mice and such can be transported in the family car fairly easily. Make sure they have enough food and water in their cages and are out of drafts or extreme temperatures. It's good to cover their cages with a cloth to keep them quiet and restful.

Remember, a long trip can be even tougher for an animal than a human. Take this into consideration when moving your pet and everyone should arrive on the other end safe and happy.

For Sale by Owner
MOVING MEMO

Books About Moving For Kids

Moving can be especially hard for young children. They may have difficulty understanding why people must leave a place they like for another place that's strange, new and different.

But if your children are like most, they'll find it easier to understand if it's told to them in the form of a story.

This is why we've compiled a list of books for children between the ages of 3 and 11. A special moving present to your child of one of these books may help them understand what moving is all about.

These books aren't fairy tales, but stories realistically told that will help your child face the problems of moving. And they're written on a level easy for your child to understand. They cover such topics as why people have to move, leaving friends behind, traveling across the country, arriving in a strange town, living in a new home, finding new things to do and see, and making new friends.

We've grouped the books according to age levels to help you select the appropriate ones. Most of these are obtainable from any large bookstore or library.

WILL YOU BE MY FRIEND? Written and illustrated by Chihiro Lwasaki. McGraw, 1970. (24 pages) Pre-2.

THAT NEW BOY. Mary Lystad, pictures by Emily McCully. Crown, 1973. (27 pages) Pre-2.

JANEY. Charlotte Zolotow, pictures by Ronald Himler. Harper, 1973. (24 pages) Pre-3.

I'M MOVING. Martha Whitmore Hickman, illustrated by Leigh Grant. Abingdon, 1974. (27 pages) Pre-3.

THE BIG HELLO. Janet Schulman, illustrated by Lillian Hoban. Morrow, 1976. (32 pages) Pre-3.

NANCY AND JEFF. Ben Farrell, illustrated by Leonard Shortall. Scholastic, 1972. (31 pages) K-3.

A & THE OR WILLIAM T.C. BAUMGARTEN COMES TO TOWN. Written and illustrated by Ellen Raskin. Atheneum, 1970. (26 pages) K-3.

MOVING DAY. Tobi Tobias, pictures by William Pene Bois. Knopf, 1976. (26 pages) K-4.

THE SHY LITTLE GIRL. Phyllis Krasilovsky, illustrated by Trina Scart Hyman. Houghton, 1970. (32 pages) 2-4.

A MONTH OF SUNDAYS. Rose Blue, illustrated by Ted Lewin. Watts, 1972. (60 pages) 4-6.

SORE LOSER. Genevieve Gray, illustrated by Beth and Jow Krush. Houghton, 1974. (74 pages) 4-6.

TONY AND ME. Alfred Slote. Lippincott, 1974. (156 pages) 4-6.

Winning with FSBO's

The key to getting an appointment with a FSBO is: stay in touch. Most agents make one contact. When 21 percent of the people decide they do need a Realtor four weeks later, they cannot remember the name of this one time visitor no matter how impressed they were. But they will remember the Realtor who provided information, maintained rapport and followed up.

4. Pursuing Expired Listings

What Is an Expired Listing?

A home that was previously listed but did not sell before the listing agreement expired. It is also a solid source of business.

What Do You Have Going for You?

You know that:

a. the seller has already made the decision to sell,

b. they are "sold" on using a real estate agent, and

c. you can assume, because the listing expired, that they are probably very motivated to sell as quickly as possible.

The Problem with Expired Listings

The house did not sell the first time around. Why? In most cases because it was over-priced. Mispricing of homes happens because of several reasons:

a. The agent may have performed a poor market analysis and misinformed the seller as to the relative value of the home. (Maybe because of over enthusiasm about some purely subjective aspects of the home—such as its decorating—which made the home seem more valuable than it actually is.)

b. The seller set the price based on what he "needed" from the sale, rather than what was a realistic price.

c. Sometimes the market changes so quickly and dramatically that a reevaluation of the price is necessary, but both seller and agent are unwilling to admit a lower price may be more appropriate.

If price kept the home from being sold, why wasn't it reduced? Probably because the real estate agent sold the seller on the wrong price and the seller was convinced his house was worth it. The agent also set the seller's expectations when he told him how successful his company was and what it would do to get the job done. The seller simply wanted the company to follow through with its promise. So when the home didn't sell, the seller assumed that the agent and company were at fault. Often you'll hear a seller say the fault was in "lack of promotion and poor advertising" or "nobody showed my house." When the problem of overpricing is addressed, the seller says he would have come down if an offer had been made. Yet, as you know, there will rarely be offers on an over-priced home.

Keep in mind this model of an expired listing:

- First, the home did not sell because of over-pricing relative to the market, location, and condition. But the seller was happy with the price either because he "needed" the money or because the agent misinformed him of the true competitive value.

- Second, the seller feels the "fault" was with the real estate company who did not promote and did not show the home.

- Finally, no matter what he says, he usually wants to sell the home. He is highly motivated to sell and would be receptive to someone who could show him how things could be done differently.

Four Steps to Rejection-Free Prospecting with Expired Listings

Step 1: Make the First Contact

Keep the model of an expired listing homeowner in mind when you make your first contact call. Don't talk about the expired listing or how you could sell the home. Your aim during the initial contact is to get an appointment to review the home, establish rapport, and show your sympathy for the person whose home is not selling.

Step 2: Contact a Number of Expired Listings

Deal in reality; chances are you will not get the listing or even the appointment from this one call—nor from two or three calls. But from five calls? Better yet, ten calls? Once you improve your odds, you increase your chances of getting a listing. One call to one person will not do it. Keep on calling.

Step 3: Guide the Conversation During the Contacts

Maintain control and guide the conversation toward your goal by being the one who asks the questions. Listen and be sincerely sympathetic. After your introduction of yourself and company, ask "Is your home still for sale?" The answer will probably be a hedge between yes and no, such as— "maybe, why, do you want to buy it?"

Regardless of this answer, immediately ask, "Would you sell it if you had someone interested in it?" A "no" reply ends the conversation, but a "yes" means the person is motivated to sell. You continue with, "Would you tell me why you think it didn't sell?" When they tell you it was a bad real estate agent, poor advertising, and no showings, do not agree that they are right in their understanding of the problem, just sympathize. "No advertising? Yes, that must have been frustrating!" Continue to ask questions about how many showings they had, any offers received. Use reflective listening to feed back their feelings to establish that you understand their feelings and are sympathetic to a frustrating situation. At about this point ask, "What's the best time for me to come and see the house?"

Whatever the response to this question, be realistic about it. Chances are the homeowner will not want you to see the house and may be so annoyed with real estate agents that he decides to really take it out on you. Remember that he is reacting to the situation and not to you. If you approach this transaction realistically you will understand there is a high probability it will not end up with an appointment and a listing. However, what you are accomplishing in making these calls is a shift of the odds in your favor. The more calls you make, the closer you are to the one that will result in an appointment to discuss the sale of a home.

Step 4: Conduct a Viewing Appointment

Begin your appointment on a positive note; find something about the home you like. The previous agent probably became negative as time wore on and tension increased. You need to come in fresh and positive. Indicate that you understand how difficult this situation is, recognize they have been burned once. Most definitely, do not give your standard presentation. Instead, tell them what you will do that is different from what the past agent did. You might suggest more open houses, or use of some special advertising offered by your firm. Discuss your referral department and your investment division or whatever your company has that is different from the first company. Based on your first conversation, you know what the other agent did and what problems the owner perceived. Stress all the ways your company approaches sales that are different from what was done before.

Finally, get down to price. Use a similar home as a model to explain and develop your method of pricing. Since you know over-pricing was the problem in the past, explain that "some people" base their price on personal "needs" rather than competitive market factors. Use comparison figures and solid facts to show how you arrive at an appropriate price for this home. Finally, make sure they agree to a realistic price, or do not take the listing. An unsaleable home costs time and money for both you and your broker. And think of the difficulty for these homeowners if their home did not sell this second time around.

Looking at the Whole Picture

Now that you have a good idea of how to prospect in the most painfree way, refer to pages 67–72 at the end of this book to help you flesh-out in more detail your picture of reality. Who are these people—your prospects? What are their expectations? Specifically, the following pages detail the finding of an in-depth consumer research report on:

- What buyers and sellers think of the real estate business
- What the major concerns of sellers are
- What the major concerns of buyers are
- Frequent complaints of buyers and sellers
- Most frequent reasons for moving

Take a few minutes now to read through pages 67 to 72, then continue with this chapter.

Prospecting Summary

What should emerge as you begin to think about the survey results is a composite picture of the buyer and seller of real estate in today's market. We have discussed what they think about the business of real estate, what is most important to sellers, what buyers are most concerned with, frequent complaints about the business, and the most common reasons for people moving. Take some time now to absorb this picture and plan your marketing strategy for producing buyers based on your knowledge of who these buyers are, where they live and where they want to live. Capitalize on your consumer awareness by incorporating the survey results into your prospecting program and listing presentation. Show the buyer and seller you know how to best satisfy his real estate needs because you have taken the time to understand what and why the needs exist.

You can no more afford *not* to know where your market is and what they are thinking than you can afford not to prospect. Hopefully, this chapter has given you the information, tools, and skills for establishing a realistic and successful prospecting program—one that responds both to *your* needs and your *prospects'* needs.

Chapter 5

Useful Tips, Lists, and Readings for Success

On the following pages are various exercises, "tips," lists, and readings that will help you get into the "Heart of Selling". . . .

About Prospecting . . . .

What Buyers and Sellers Think about the Real Estate Business

1. Most buyers and sellers do not regard the selection of a real estate broker as an area of concern.

Consumers believe most real estate agents are the same; none better, none worse. They do not care to compare companies, since they expect to find them all the same.

2. The seller, to a large degree, makes the choice of an agent on the basis of personal acquaintances rather than by shopping around.

This is why prospecting is so important. If you can expand your sphere of social acquaintances through prospecting and farming, you will greatly increase your odds of being selected as the buyer's or seller's agent.

3. Most buyers and sellers are not impressed with the size of a firm.

People list with a person—not a company. They are interested in doing business with you. As long as your company maintains ethical and professional standards, most people do not see any direct benefit to them because of the size of your firm.

4. The fear of the unknown is one of the buyers' main concerns when purchasing a new home.

This fear about what "could happen" in a real estate transaction keeps many people from deciding to buy. It is imperative that you explain the steps involved in buying a house so that they will feel informed and comfortable. When they are comfortable, they are more receptive to the home and the conditions of purchase.

5. The majority of sellers move within nineteen miles of their previous home.

This is the reason we should spend a great deal of time prospecting. If we realize that 66 percent of all buyers come from within a nineteen mile radius of the home they buy, we should spend more time prospecting the area for buyers rather than waiting for a buyer to "transfer in" from out of town. Are you and your broker spending most of your efforts within this nineteen mile area?

6. The majority of sellers do not feel very knowledgeable about the sale of their home.

This may seem contrary to your experience with sellers—many of whom give the impression that they think they know more than you. The reality is that they do not think *you* know very much. The image of real estate as a profession is unfortunately not very high. They don't know that it takes more than one 30-hour course to produce a dedicated, educated professional—like you.

7. The majority of sellers select an individual agent rather than selecting a firm first.

Sellers prefer to deal with someone they know, no matter how remote the contact or how little they really know about the agent. People still deal with the person before the company. This doesn't mean that the company with whom you're associated is irrelevant but that it is with you they choose to list their home.

8. Among people who both bought and sold houses in the past year, more actually bought their new house before selling their old house.

Be aware of this when on a listing presentation. Even though a client may have just listed his present home, he may be receptive to suggestions about a new home. Be prepared to turn the listing presentation into a sales presentation.

9. The majority of home sellers did not consult more than one agent before listing their house.

Seventy-eight percent of the people in the survey talked to only one sales agent before listing their home for sale! Success in real estate means making the contact, seeing the people. The odds are with you that you will get the listing if you get there first and have some product knowledge. That is why prospecting is so important; if you prospect, you will be there at the right time.

10. For the most part, both buyers and sellers were very satisfied with the individual agents they used.

This is because they did not expect much in the first place. The professional who does a good job can do much towards elevating the image of Realtors—and of securing his place in the buyer's or seller's mind as an agent who knows his business. This is especially important for repeat business and as a source of future referrals.

What Are the Major Concerns of Sellers?

1. Price

The selling price of the home is the main concern among sellers. This is an area of possible confusion, misinformation, and seller discomfort. Plan your presentation with this in mind. Remember: discuss the entire pricing process using a model unrelated to your client's home as you explain market analysis procedures. Elaborate on possible sellling problems based on faulty pricing strategies. Use of an impersonal model for discussion helps the seller understand the pricing process before he becomes personally involved with the pricing of his own home. Take extra time and care to handle properly this number one concern of your seller.

2. Net Sales Proceeds

After selling price, the next most important concern of the seller is how much money will be realized from the sale. This is nothing new; everyone tells the seller how much money he can expect to "walk away with." But take the telling one step further by including the net sales proceeds figure in your pricing presentation. Acknowledge its importance to your seller by clearly highlighting the process and the approximate dollar figure resulting. This insures your seller is informed and in agreement with your figures.

3. Timeliness

Sellers are concerned that their house sell quickly and in coordination with their moving plans—date of transfer, closing on the next house. Make sure you ask questions about what the seller's time needs are. Then discuss your marketing strategy in relation to these needs—how your referral network or marketing program will help assure a timely sale.

4. Closing Procedures

Just because sellers were once buyers does not mean they understand the closing process. Tell them what happens from the time an offer is made to the day they receive a check at the closing. Take them through the steps, alleviating the fear of the unknown along the way. Make them comfortable by explaining what will happen and by showing them you are in control to assure that the process goes smoothly.

What Are the Major Concerns of Buyers?

1. Price

Buyers tell us price is more important to them than location. If the price is right it compensates for a second-choice location. The price of a home can always be adjusted; the location never can. Concentrate on showings in affordable locations.

2. Condition

Still more important than location is the condition of the home. Do you take the time to be responsive to this concern by discussing the age of the home and appliances or the possibility of purchasing a home warranty? As part of your listing presentation, do you ask the seller questions relating to the home's overall condition? An excellent listing sales tool is to share the survey results indicating buyers' concerns with the condition of the property. Ask the seller to list positives—and negatives—relating to the condition of the home. This approach shows both buyer and seller that you understand and are responsive to their needs and concerns.

3. Location

Know the area and make sure you point out the important aspects of the neighborhood: location of schools, shops, parks. In the listing presentation, demonstrate to the seller that you know the area so he will be confident of your ability to respond to a prospective buyer concerned about location.

4. Financing

People want to know what their down payment will be. But they might not know that you can tell them about the service charge, estimate their taxes, quote the monthly payment, and tell them exactly how the financing process works. Explain the whole process in detail so they are comfortable with what is going to happen.

Frequent Complaints of Buyers and Sellers

1. "Too much pressure."

Clients too often fear a loss of control when dealing with a sales person viewed as pushy and aggressive. In reality, 44 percent of all sales agents quit after the first objection; 92 percent quit after the fourth objection. Yet the average buyer objects six times before buying. If people think a salesperson is going to be pushy, that is the reality you must confront. Do not avoid this problem; address it by a simple statement that your aim is to provide a service and your intention is not to be overly aggressive. If they feel you are coming on too strong—ask them to please tell you.

2. "Salespersons don't keep me informed."

Buyers and sellers are afraid that after they have "signed on the dotted line," they will not hear from you again until closing when you collect your commission. Communicate with your clients regularly. Even no news is good news to a buyer who is wondering if any problems have developed in his deal. Note: while this may sound contradictory to the concern that you may be too aggressive, there *is* a difference between bothering someone and keeping them informed.

3. "Salespersons won't tell me about the 'hidden costs.' "

People fear a lack of full disclosure. They have heard you are likely to hide something from them until it is "too late." The best way to prove your openness is to confront this preconception. Tell your client you understand he may be concerned about "hidden costs." Enumerate in writing all the costs involved in a real estate transaction. Reinforce your commitment to keep him informed should some future event alter these figures. Explain all costs fully and in detail.

4. "I don't want to see the wrong home, the wrong size, and at the wrong price."

People are afraid they will have to trudge through home after home searching for the one just right for their family. Listen to the needs of your buyer instead of his description of the house in his mind's eye. When you identify his needs you will be able to adjust his picture to your picture—based on market availability—or what style home will answer these needs. Poor qualifying comes from poor communication.

Most Frequent Reasons for Moving

1. Buy Instead of Rent

The number one source of buyers is renters. This fact should suggest a marketing approach aimed at establishing contact with apartment dwellers. If your area is mainly a single family suburb, go into the city where more people live in apartments. You will find most apartment dwellers do not buy houses because they simply do not know how. The information you provide by a regular series of mailings and a routine of personal contact will be well received.

2. Larger Home; Moving Up

Be aware of the place your home holds on the upward mobility scale. If you are trying to sell a home suitable for a young, small family, concentrate your marketing efforts among apartment renters. If the home is large with many extra features, logic suggests your buyer may live in a subdivision with homes slightly smaller and less customized. These are the people most likely to be "moving up" to the larger home.

3. Job Change

4. Better Neighborhood

You Are What You Choose to Be

All things are simple when you reduce them to fundamentals. It's the untangling, the reducing that's complicated. Get rid of the clutter.

Do you choose to be successful? If you do, you will be doing the following on a regular basis:

Prospecting—

(1) Personal Referrals

(2) Farming

(3) FSBO

(4) Expired Listings

Learning—

(1) Communication Skills

(2) Technical Skills

Managing yourself effectively

Developing your self-image

Accepting responsibility for your success.

Or Do You Choose to Be Unsuccessful?

Starting late (after 9:00 A.M.)

Blaming everything and everybody for Your failures:

>   (1) Market Conditions

>   (2) Broker

>   (3) Advertising Program

>   (4) Bad Luck

Taking long lunches (over 45 minutes)

Not investing in success

>   (1) Personal Items for Prospects

>   (2) Seminars, Tapes, Books

Hanging around the office

Working with paper instead of with people

About Self Image . . .

Do you see yourself successful?

- $2,000,000 producer
- Manager
- Broker-owner
- Trainer
- Risk taker

Take risks—success or failure isn't the reward—taking the risk is. Let your emotions flow.

A ship in a harbor is safe, but that is not what ships are built for.

or do you see yourself unsuccessful?

- Mediocre producer
- Struggling
- Never winning sales awards
- Afraid of rejection

When handling little failures in life remember the choice is yours.

Frustration triggers anxiety

Anxiety triggers hostility

Hostility triggers energy

Energy can be

Negative or positive

Symptoms of a Poor Self-Image

- Sloppy appearance
- Weak or uncertain voice
- Wears "protective masks"
- Unable to admit mistakes
- Tries to be "better than" by making others "wrong" or "less than"
- Jealous, envious, and suspicious
- Preoccupied with shame, guilt, and regret
- Needs to be liked and accepted by everyone

What Can You Do to Change?

Ideas for building a stronger self-image:

Become physically fit:

(1) Exercise.

(2) Stop smoking.

(3) Lose weight.

For every inch your waistline exceeds the size of your chest, you can deduct two years from how long you can expect to live.
—Metropolitan Life Insurance Company

Be cheerful and make others feel important. Happiness is contagious; so is negativism.

Visualize yourself as a success. Accentuate your assets.

(1) Prospect 2–3 hours each day.

(2) Start your work day early (8:00 A.M.)

Learn something new every day—

> (1) Read books.

> (2) Listen to tapes.

> (3) Attend seminars.

Create something.

Be nice to someone.

End each day with a win!

Is Changing Easy?

- Changing is difficult—it doesn't take miracles; it takes work.
- You must believe you are going to change your self-image.
- You can be happy if you really want to be.
- You will make mistakes in your self-image development, but stay with it—it's worth it.
- You won't succeed all the time. No one is perfect. Perfectionism is an enemy to success.
- Do not create an omnipotent, fictitious self that is as harmful as a negative self. You are what you are—unique. Find out what is best and use it.
- Most people decline physically and mentally after high school and college—only 5 percent continue to grow at the same or greater pace.
- We've become watchers instead of doers.
- We have a tendency towards creative avoidance (figuring out why we can't do something).
- People see, hear, and read what they want to see, hear, and read. They develop blind spots (creatively) for the rest.
- Cognitive dissonance says that man cannot have conflictive thoughts so he works for harmony, sometimes even at his expense.
- A weak self-image keeps us in our comfort zone. Good self-image allows us to go higher and poor self-image restricts us.
- Ask yourself if you put yourself into uncomfortable situations—this is many times a sign of growth.
- The first year of personal growth is difficult and slow because you are not a total believer. After that the growth can be tremendous.
- Set positive habit patterns which will lead you to your new goals.

Activities to Develop Your Self-Image

List the following

3 positive qualities I have.

____

_______________________________________ Example:

_______________________________________ Hard-working

3 positive experiences I have had.

____

_______________________________________ Example: That

_______________________________________ listing I got

3 potential strengths I need to develop.

____

_______________________________________ Example:

_______________________________________ Prospecting

3 things I would like to be rid of.

_______________________________________ Example: Nega-

_______________________________________ tive people in

_______________________________________ my life

3 reasons why I want to change.

_______________________________________ Example: I want

_______________________________________ to feel good

_______________________________________ about myself.

About Communications . . .

The A.R.C. Triangle—A Communications Tool

When your success depends on effective communication you cannot take the chance of being a non-responsive communicator. A convenient tool for discovering and analyzing why ineffective communication occurs is the ARC Triangle.

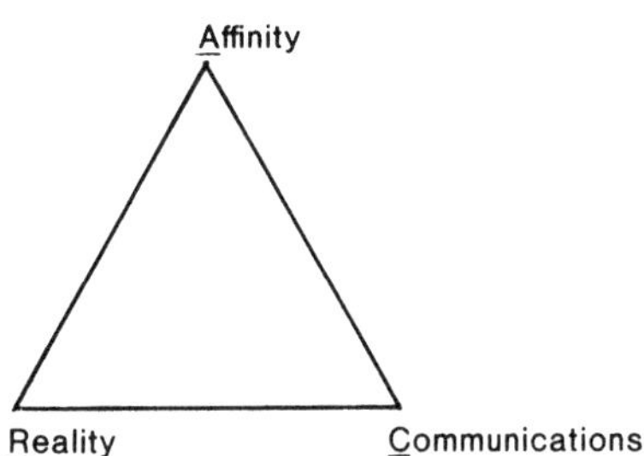

In every interaction there are three common components which must be positive in order for you to guide the conversation to a favorable conclusion. Review your interaction with buyers and sellers on the three prongs of the ARC triangle to see where effective communication stopped and to learn how to avoid this in future transactions. Look at how you:

Establish Affinity

Did the people with whom you were dealing like you? Were you able to establish some common point of view, a similar way of responding to something with which your clients could agree and could likewise respond positively? Decide if your expectations of this meeting interfered with establishing this rapport. It is just as much a mistake to assume everyone will automatically like you as it is to assume they will not like you. Either extreme must be dealt with in the reality of the actual situation—you cannot please all of the people. Being aware of this possibility means that you will take the time to do something to develop this affinity rather than taking it for granted. Do not belabor the effort; just pause long enough before you "get down to business" to make a sincere effort to meet and know these people. Chances are that your effort will be understood, appreciated, and rewarded with a similar effort to know and relate to you.

Respond to Their Reality

Are you talking to people on the basis of their needs and wants—or yours? Are you so impressed with a house that you focus on how to get the top dollar for it and tune out the fact that the first concern of these sellers is speed because they need to move within a month's time? Take the time to understand their reality—what is really important to them. Listen and understand where they are to avoid imposing your reality onto them.

Communicate

Can you clearly, logically and effectively tell your clients exactly what you can do for them? Have you sufficiently organized and prepared your presentation so it flows smoothly? Do you have a sound understanding of what these people need to hear in order to make a potentially confusing proposal easy to follow?

Saying that everyone can communicate is not to say that everyone does it effectively. Communication is an art which requires preparation and practice. The only good thing about an unsuccessful effort at communication is its potential to teach you how to improve. The next time you plan a presentation, think about the interlinking components of the ARC Triangle. Examine the interaction of affinity, reality, and communication (your strengths/weaknesses) to understand how to be a more effective communicator.

Ten Tips for Good Listening

1. Stop talking—there is no way that you can listen if you are talking.

2. Put the talker at ease—help him to feel that he is free to talk.

3. Show him that you want to listen—look and act interested.

4. Remove distractions—do not doodle, shuffle papers, or constantly move around in your chair.

5. Empathize—put yourself in his place so you see his point of view.

6. Be patient—allow plenty of time and do not interrupt.

7. Hold your temper—anger can get in the way of hearing what the other person is saying.

8. Avoid argument and criticism—this causes the other person to be defensive.

9. Ask questions—this encourages the other person and shows you are listening.

10. Stop talking—this is the most important way to make sure you listen enough.

About Goal Setting . . .

Questions to Ask Myself at the End of the Day

- Is it clear to me what I wanted to accomplish? (goals)
- Did I work effectively to be the success I want to be or did I waste time?
- Did I reward myself for productive experiences for which I was responsible for during the day?
- Am I being too harsh on myself for not being perfect in accordance with what I want to do?
- Did I laugh?

How I Will Work Towards Fulfillment

- I will develop good habits through hard work.
- I will work on my self-image regularly.
- I will laugh more.
- I will help others, but not at the expense of my self-image.
- I will do things that I enjoy, not what others want me to do.
- I will confront things because I know I can handle anything I can confront.

> Courage is resistance to fear, mastery of fear, not absence of fear.
>
> —Mark Twain

- I will set goals that are definite and realistic.
- I will believe in myself and my uniqueness.

The "Positive Affirmation"

An affirmation is a powerful tool for programming the mind. Example: "I feel warm and loving toward myself, for I am a unique and precious person, always doing the best that I can."

Using the affirmation:

(1) Relax and breathe deeply.

(2) Is morning or night time best for you?

(3) Repeat during the day.

(4) Believe in what you say.

Take direct action:

(1) Select your area of greatest need.

(2) Write your own affirmation.

(3) Repeat it a **minimum** of ten times per day.

(4) Recognize your growth.

(5) Enjoy the victory.

(6) Continue the process.

The following are examples of **AFFIRMATIONS.** Feel free to formulate your own or change these to fit your personal needs. You will find that the more comfortable you feel with an **AFFIRMATION,** the better it will work for you.

1. I am solely responsible for my own life and wellbeing. (If I am not happy and at peace with myself it is up to me, and me alone, to discover the causes and take appropriate action.)

2. I have the innate authority to take full charge of my own life—to think, say, and do anything I choose.

3. There is a price exacted for everything I do. It is up to me to determine such price and intelligently decide whether or not I am able and willing to pay it.

4. I have the right and freedom to make mistakes, to be defeated, to fail, for I can do only as well as my current awareness permits.

5. I can do anything I want, but what I want is determined by my awareness.

6. My fundamental motivation is to "feel good" mentally, physically, and emotionally—to resolve or satisfy my unfulfilled needs and desires.

7. All "oughts," "shoulds," and "musts" are irrelevent and meaningless for any action my prevailing awareness does not, or cannot, motivate me to take.

8. I invariably do the best I can possibly do at the time.

9. We must pay a "price" for our every act, whether "good" or "bad."

10. There is no valid basis for resistance to anything I cannot change. (Such resistance causes only turmoil and resentment.)

11. Worry, resistance, and resentment are both futile and destructive to one's well-being.

12. I am the center of my universe; my world revolves around me.

13. I am a genuine "success" to the degree that I feel warm and loving toward myself.

14. I have no need to "prove" myself since my very existence proves my innate worth and importance.

15. Comparing myself with another's personality, conduct, or accomplishments as a gauge of my worth is absolutely meaningless. For no two people have had the same heritage and total life experience.

16. My physical well-being is of critical importance to my emotional well-being. Otherwise, I would not have the energy to support my motivation, however wise it might be.

Self-Exercise—What Matters?

DIRECTIONS: Take five minutes to write down everything you can think of and "feel" that matters to you—personally and professionally. Don't worry about the order or their importance—just let yourself keep writing.

WHAT MATTERS TO ME IS:

Self-Exercise—Setting Priorities

DIRECTIONS: Using the list of thirteen life priority categories below:

1. Assign a priority to each (1 to 13—highest = 1; lowest = 13)

2. Match the various activities that you listed in the previous exercise (What Matters to Me) to the categories you just assigned priorities to.

LIFE CATEGORY	PRIORITY	LIFE CATEGORY	PRIORITY
1. Service to others		8. Security	
2. Power		9. Independence	
3. Pleasure/Fun		10. Recognition	
4. Religion		11. Health	
5. Morality		12. Love/Family	
6. Income/Wealth		13. Aesthetics	
7. Challenging Opportunities			

Self-Exercise—Writing Goals

Directions: Based on your priorities—set your goals for this year. (Refer to the Components of Meaningful Goals, page 26.)

When you have written all your goals:

1. Assign rankings of A, B, or C (see explanation on pp. 29–30).

2. Within those rankings assign priorities (A1, A2, etc.)

3. Use the next page to list what you are going to do over the next seven days to get closer to accomplishing your goals.

To Do List

WEEK OF: ____

DAY	**TO DO**	**PRIORITY**

Commitment/Action Plans

    (1) When I experience failure, I will

____

____

____

    (2) To improve my self-image, I will

____

____

____

    (3) My major goals for next year are

____

____

____

    (4) For business, I will work on three high priority items which are

____

__________________________________ Example:

__________________________________ Prospecting

And I will stay away from these three low priority items

__________________________________ Example:

__________________________________ Socializing

__________________________________ in the office

(5) In order to become a better communicator I will

____

____

____

(6) I will take control of my own life and will not
allow the following people to "pull my strings:"

____

____

____

When I fill in these pages I will reward myself by

____

____

Make sure that this is truly a reward and in harmony with your objectives. That is, don't reward yourself with a piece of pie if one of your goals is to lose weight.

Only those who understand and live through a positive self-image will continue in directions they know are right, even when numerous obstacles are encountered along the way.

I believe in the Individual and the Individual must believe in Himself.

The common idea that success spoils people by making them vain, egotistic, and self-complacent is erroneous: on the contrary, it makes them for the most part humble, tolerant and kind. Failure makes people bitter and cruel.

W. Somerset Maugham.

Conclusion

Hopefully the ideas presented in this book will help you identify and attain what you really want in life. Real estate sales provides an outstanding opportunity to create the life you want, in the way you want. However, this is not without hard work, careful scrutiny of yourself and others, change when appropriate, and constant reexamination of where you are, what you want, and how and when you're going to get there.

You *can* be, have, and do what you want. Don't hesitate—start now. Begin with the goals and plans you've just worked out, with some fresh ideas concerning communication and your feelings about yourself, and finally with some proven techniques for rejection-free prospecting.

It's all there for you—along with my very best wishes for success.

Jim DuVal

For information on products mentioned in this book, or for a brochure of our product line, please contact

Creative Real Estate Services
1114 Pennsylvania NE
Albuquerque, N.M. 87110

(505)255-7007